Source Readings in Music History

Books by Oliver Strunk

Source Readings in Music History

Essays on Music in The Western World

Essays on Music in The Byzantine World

SOURCE READINGS IN MUSIC HISTORY

The Romantic Era

Selected and Annotated by

OLIVER STRUNK

PRINCETON UNIVERSITY

W · W · NORTON & COMPANY · INC · New York

PRINTED IN THE UNITED STATES OF AMERICA

7 8 9 0

Throughout the book, small letters refer to notes by the authors of the individual selections, arabic numerals to editor's notes. The abbreviation "*S.R.*" followed by a Roman numeral refers to another volume in the *Source Readings in Music History*.

Contents

I

LITERARY FORERUNNERS OF MUSICAL ROMANTICISM

II

COMPOSER-CRITICS OF THE NINETEENTH CENTURY

Preface to the Five-Volume Edition

My *Source Readings in Music History*, a music-historical companion running to more than 900 pages and extending from classical antiquity through the romantic era, was originally published in 1950. That it is now being reissued in parts is due to a recognition, shared by the publishers and myself, that the usefulness of the book would be considerably enhanced if the readings for the single periods were also available separately and in a handier form. From the first, the aim had been to do justice to every age without giving to any a disproportionate share of the space. Thus the book has lent itself naturally to a division into parts, approximately equal in length, each part complete in itself. For use in the classroom, the advantages of the present edition are sufficiently obvious. For the casual reader, whose interest in the history of music is not likely to be all-inclusive, it will have other advantages, equally obvious. In the meantime, the original edition in one volume will remain in print and will be preferred by those who wish to have the whole between two covers, to be able to refer readily from one part of the book to another, and to be able to consult a single index.

In reprinting here the foreword to the edition of 1950, I have retained only those paragraphs that apply in some measure to all parts of the whole.

O. S.

Rome, 1965

Foreword

THIS BOOK began as an attempt to carry out a suggestion made in 1929 by Carl Engel in his *Views and Reviews*—to fulfil his wish for "a living record of musical personalities, events, conditions, tastes . . . a history of music faithfully and entirely carved from contemporary accounts." It owes something, too, to the well-known compilations of Kinsky and Schering and rather more, perhaps, to Andrea della Corte's *Antologia della storia della musica* and to an evaluation of this, its first model, by Alfred Einstein.

In its present form, however, it is neither the book that Engel asked for nor a literary anthology precisely comparable to the pictorial and musical ones of Kinsky and Schering, still less an English version of its Italian predecessor, with which it no longer has much in common. It departs from Engel's ideal scheme in that it has, at bottom, a practical purpose—to make conveniently accessible to the teacher or student of the history of music those things which he must eventually read. Historical documents being what they are, it inevitably lacks the seemingly unbroken continuity of Kinsky and Schering; at the same time, and for the same reason, it contains far more that is unique and irreplaceable than either of these. Unlike della Corte's book it restricts itself to historical documents as such, excluding the writing of present-day historians; aside from this, it naturally includes more translations, fewer original documents, and while recognizing that the somewhat limited scope of the *Antologia* was wholly appropriate in a book on music addressed to Italian readers, it seeks to take a broader view.

That, at certain moments in its development, music has been a subject of widespread and lively contemporary interest, calling forth a flood of documentation, while at other moments, perhaps not less critical, the records are either silent or unrevealing—this is in no way remarkable, for it is inherent in the very nature of music, of letters, and of history. The beginnings of the classical symphony and string quartet passed virtually unnoticed as developments without interest for the literary man; the beginnings of the opera and cantata, developments which concerned him immediately and deeply, were heralded and reviewed in documents so numerous that, even in a book of this size, it has been possible to include only the most significant. Thus, as already suggested, a documentary history of music cannot properly exhibit even the degree of continuity that is possible for an iconographic one or a collection of musical monuments, still less the degree expected of an interpretation. For this reason, too, I have rejected the simple chronological arrangement as inappropriate and misleading and have preferred to allow the documents to arrange themselves naturally under the various topics chronologically ordered in the Table of Contents and the book itself, some of these admirably precise, others perhaps rather too inclusive. As Engel shrewdly anticipated, the frieze has turned out to be incomplete, and I have left the gaps unfilled, as he wished.

For much the same reason, I have not sought to give the book a spurious unity by imposing upon it a particular point of view. At one time it is the musician himself who has the most revealing thing to say; at another time he lets someone else do the talking for him. And even when the musician speaks it is not always the composer who speaks most clearly; sometimes it is the theorist, at other times the performer. If this means that few readers will find the book uniformly interesting, it ought also to mean that "the changing patterns of life," as Engel called them, will be the more fully and the more faithfully reflected.

It was never my intention to compile a musical Bartlett, and I have accordingly sought, wherever possible, to include the complete text of the selection chosen, or—failing this—the complete text of a continuous, self-contained, and independently intelligible passage or series of passages, with or without regard for the chapter divisions of the original. But in a few cases I have made cuts to eliminate digressions or to avoid needless repetitions of things equally well said by earlier writers; in other cases the excessive length and involved construction of the original has forced me to abridge, reducing the scale of the whole while retaining the essential continuity of the argument. All cuts are clearly indicated, either by a row of dots or in annotations.

Without the lively encouragement and patient sympathy of the late William Warder Norton my work on this book would never have been begun. Nor is it at all likely that I would ever have finished it without the active collaboration of my father, William Strunk, Jr., Emeritus Professor of English at Cornell University, whose expert assistance and sound advice were constantly at my disposal during the earlier stages of its preparation and who continued to follow my work on it with the keenest interest until 1946, the year of his death. A considerable number of the translations now published for the first time are largely his work and there are few to which he did not make some improving contribution.

My warmest thanks are due to Professor Otto Kinkeldey, of Cornell University, and to Professor Alfred Einstein, of Smith College, for their extraordinary kindness in consenting to read the entire book in proof and for the many indispensable corrections and suggestions that they have sent me; again to Alfred Einstein, and to Paul Hindemith, for a number of constructive recommendations which grew out of their experiments with sections of the manuscript in connection with their teaching; likewise to my old friends Paul Lang, Arthur Mendel, and Erich Hertzmann, who have always been ready to listen and to advise.

Acknowledgment is due, also, to Dr. Dragan Plamenac, who prepared the greater number of the brief biographical notes which accompany the single readings; to two of my students—Philip Keppler, Jr., who relieved me of some part of the proofreading and J. W. Kerman, who prepared the index; to Gordon Mapes, for his careful work on the autographing of the musical examples; and to Miss Katherine Barnard, Miss Florence Williams, and the entire staff of W. W. Norton & Co., Inc., for their unflagging interest and innumerable kindnesses.

OLIVER STRUNK

The American Academy in Rome

I

Literary Forerunners of Musical Romanticism

1. Jean Paul

"The highest criticism is that which leaves an impression identical with the one called forth by the thing criticized. In this sense Jean Paul, with a poetic companion-piece, can perhaps contribute more to the understanding of a symphony or fantasy by Beethoven, without even speaking of the music, than a dozen of those little critics of the arts who lean their ladders against the Colossus and take its exact measurements."

Strange to say, this observation of Schumann's is not altogether wide of the mark. A self-taught amateur whose piano-playing did not go beyond the improvisation of extravagant rhapsodies, Jean Paul responded almost as a clairvoyant to the poetic side of musical composition; a musical writer who never wrote on music, he exerted a compelling influence on the music and musical criticism of his time. By 1800, thanks to the musical episodes and allusions in his early novels, his name had become so closely identified with music in the minds of his readers that a sentimental ode by Andreas Kretschmer could win immediate and widespread popularity simply by being printed under the title "Jean Paul's Favorite Song." Two well-known writers on music sought him out and recorded their impressions of his personality—J. F. Reichardt, who spent an evening with him in 1796, and Ludwig Rellstab, who called on him in 1822 with a letter from Tieck. For many of his contemporaries he was the literary counterpart of Beethoven. August Lewald, who knew them both, found that they had much in common and reports that the resemblance extended even to physical characteristics. "Beethoven was somewhat smaller," he wrote in 1836, "but one noticed at once the same powerful nature, the same indifference to external appearance, the same kindliness, the same simplicity and cordiality. If we look at their works we find the same profundity, the same sharp characterization, the same painting of details; quiet states of temperament are described and sudden outbursts of extreme passion; ideas that might have been drawn from the most commonplace reality alternate with the highest flights into the sublime. I am confident that I can rediscover in Beethoven's symphonies the Swedish country parson's Sunday (*Flegeljahre*), the unfortunate's dream (*Herbst-Blumine*), Natalia Aquilana's letter (*Siebenkäs*), and the most magnificent episodes of the *Titan*. Only in Jean Paul's improvisation, however, did his kinship with Beethoven become truly evident."

The son of a musician whose father had been a musician before him, Jean Paul (properly Johann Paul Friedrich Richter) was born at Wunsiedel in the Bavarian Fichtelgebirge on March 21, 1763. After attending the university in Leipzig he lived for a time in Hof and later in Weimar; in 1804 he settled in Bayreuth, where he continued a resident until his death on November 14, 1825. Two of Jean Paul's shorter writings, *Quintus Fixlein* and *Des Feldpredigers Schmelzle Reise nach Flätz*, were translated into English by Carlyle.

From *the* Vorschule der Aesthetik [1]

[*2d ed., 1813*]

22. THE NATURE OF ROMANTIC POETRY

THE SOUTHERN AND THE NORTHERN DISTINGUISHED

"THE ORIGIN and character of all recent poetry is so readily derived from Christianity that one could quite as well call this poetry Christian as romantic." With this assertion the author of the present paragraphs opened fire some years ago; [2] refuted and instructed, however, by more than one worthy critic of the arts, he has felt called upon to alter some details, removing them as one might remove a suburb to protect a fortification or a city as a whole. The first question is: Wherein does the romantic style [a] differ from the Greek? Greek images, stimuli, motives, sensations, characters, even technical restrictions are easily transplanted into a romantic poem without the latter's surrendering on this account its universal spirit; in the other direction, however, the transplanted romantic stimulus finds no congenial place in the Greek art work, unless it be a stimulus of the exalted sort, and then only because the exalted, like a borderline divinity, links the romantic with the antique. Even the so-called modern irregularity, for example that of the Italian opera or the Spanish comedy, may—since mere technique has not the power to

---

a Schiller calls it the *modern*, as though everything written since Grecian times were modern and new, irrespective of whether one or two thousand years old; likewise the *sentimental*, an epithet which the romanticists Ariosto and Cervantes would not have taken over-seriously. [In Schiller's "Über naive und sentimentalische Dichtung," first published in *Die Horen* for 1795 and 1796.—Ed.]

1 Text: *Sämtliche Werke*, I. Abteilung, XI (Weimar, 1935), 75–81. I have made some use of the notes of Eduard Berend, the editor of this volume of Jean Paul's collected works.

2 The first edition of the *Vorschule* was published in 1804.

divide the spiritual sphere of poetry into an old world and an American new one—be pervaded and animated with the spirit of Antiquity; this is nicely supported by the observation of Bouterwek,[3] who says that Italian poetry, for all its lack of ideas, through its clarity, simplicity, and grace follows and approaches the Greek model more nearly than any other modern sort, and this though the Italian forms have traveled further from the Greek than either the German or the English. And with this correct observation Bouterwek refutes that other one of his,[4] according to which romanticism is precisely to be found in an un-Greek community of the serious, indeed tragic, and the comic. For this is as little a necessary characteristic of the romantic, where it is often absent, as its opposite is of the antique, where it is frequently present, for example, in Aristophanes, who sternly and crassly blends the exaltation of the choruses with the humiliation of the gods themselves, as though blending an intensification of an emotion with its comic relaxation.

Rather let us ask feeling why, for example, it calls even a countryside romantic. A statue, through its sharp, closed outlines, excludes everything romantic; painting begins to approach it more closely through its groups of human figures and, without them, attains it in landscapes, for example in those of Claude.[5] A Dutch garden seems only to deny everything romantic, but an English one, reaching out into the indefinite landscape, can surround us with a romantic countryside, that is, with a background of imagination set free amid the beautiful. What is it, further, that confers on the following poetic examples their romantic stamp? In the tragedy *Numantia* of Cervantes, the citizens, in order not to fall victims to hunger and the Romans, dedicate themselves in a body to a common death. When they have carried this out and the empty city is strewn with corpses and funeral pyres, Fame appears on the walls and proclaims to the enemy the suicide of the city and the future brilliance of Spain. Again, in the midst of Homer, the romantic passage in which Jupiter surveys from Mount Olympus, at one time and under one sun, the warlike upwrought Trojan plain and the far Arcadian meadows, filled with men of peace.[6] Or, although it sparkles less brightly, the passage in Schiller's *Tell* in which the eye of the poet sweeps down from the towering chain of mountain peaks to the long, laughing cornfields of the German lowlands.[7] In all these examples, the decisive element is not that of *exaltation*, which, as we

---

3 *Geschichte der Poesie und Beredsamkeit* (Göttingen, 1801–19), II, 544.
4 In his review of the *Vorschule*.
5 Claude Lorrain (Claude Gellée), French landscape-painter of the seventeenth century.

6 *Iliad*, xiii, 1.
7 *Wilhelm Tell*, III, iii.

have said, readily flows over into the romantic, but that of *expanse*.[8]
Romanticism is beauty without bounds—the beautiful infinite, just as
there is an exalted infinite. Thus Homer, in the example we have given,
is romantic, while in the passage in which Ajax prays to the gods from
the darkened battlefield, asking only for light,[9] he is merely exalted. It
is more than a simile to call romanticism the wavelike ringing of a string
or bell, in which the tone-wave fades into ever further distances, finally
losing itself in us so that, while already silent without, it still resounds
within. In the same way, the moonlight is at once a romantic image and
a romantic example. To the Greeks, who defined things sharply, the half-
light of the romantic was so remote and foreign that even Plato, so much
the poet and so close to the Christian upheaval, in treating a genuinely
romantic-infinite subject—the relation of our petty finite world to the
resplendent hall and starry roof of the infinite—expresses it only through
the confined and angular allegory of a cave, from out which we chain-
bound ones see passing in procession the shadows of the true beings who
move behind us.[10]

If poetry is prophecy, then romanticism is being aware of a larger future
than there is room for here below; romantic blossoms float about us, just
as wholly unfamiliar sorts of seeds drifted through the all-connecting
sea from the New World, even before it had been discovered, to the Nor-
wegian shore.

Who is the author of this romanticism? Not in every land and century
the Christian religion, to be sure; to this divine mother, however, all its
others are somehow related. Two un-Christian varieties of romanticism,
historically and climatically independent of one another, are those of
India and the Edda. Old Norse romanticism, bordering more nearly on
the exalted, finds for the ghostly Orcus in the shadowy realm of its
climatically darkened and awe-inspiring natural environment, in its nights
and on its mountains, a boundless spirit world in which the narrow sensual
world dissolves and sinks from sight; here Ossian [b] belongs, with his

---

b Great as are the advantages of Ahlwardt's
translation, thanks to the discovery of the purer
text, it seems to me nonetheless that far too little
of the praise that is its due has been accorded to
the lightness, the fidelity, and the euphonies of
the translation by Jung. [James Macpherson's
pretended translations from "Ossian" had been
translated into German by F. W. Jung in 1808
and by C. W. Ahlwardt in 1811.—Ed.]

8 For further illustrations of the application of
this thoroughly romantic principle, see the ex-
cerpts from Jean Paul's *Hesperus* (p. 29 below:
"The harmonica tones flowed like radiating
echoes," or p. 33: "And thou, reëchoing sound

of the harmonica") or, for examples drawn from
music, Liszt's *Ce qu'on entend sur la montagne*
(after Victor Hugo) or Wagner's
    In des Wonnemeeres
    wogendem Schwall,
    in der Duft-Wellen
    tönendem Schall,
    in des Welt-Atems
    wehendem All—
    ertrinken—
    versinken—
    unbewusst—
    höchste Lust!

9 *Iliad*, xvii, 645.
10 *Republic*, vii (514–521B).

evening and night pieces in which the heavenly nebulous stars of the past stand twinkling above the thick nocturnal mist of the present; only in the past does he find future and eternity.

Everything in his poem is music, but it is a distant and hence a doubled music, grown faint in endless space like an echo that enchants, not through its crudely faithful reproduction of a sound, but through its attenuating mitigation of it.

Hindu romanticism has as its element an all-enlivening religion which, through animism, has broken away the confines from the sensual world; this world has become as expansive as the spirit world itself, yet it is filled, not with mischievous spirits, but with cajoling ones, and earth and sky reach out toward one another as they do at sea. To the Hindu a flower is more alive than to the Norseman a man. To this, add the climate, that voluptuous bridal night of nature, and the Hindu himself, who, like the bee reposing in the honey-filled calix of the tulip, is swung to and fro by tepid west winds and takes his rest in a delightful rocking. Precisely for this reason, Hindu romanticism had inevitably to lose itself more and more in the magic of the senses, and if the moonlight and the echo are characteristics and images of other romantic kinds, the Hindu kind may be characterized by its dark perfume, the more so since this so frequently pervades its poetry and its life.

Through its predilection for the exalted and the lyric, through its incapacity for drama and characterization—above all, through its Oriental mode of thought and feeling—Oriental poetry is related less to the Greek than to the romantic. This mode of thought and feeling—namely, the sense of the mortal futility of our night's shadows (shadows cast, not by a sun, but as though by moon and stars—shadows that the meager light itself resembles); the sense that we live our day of life under a total eclipse filled with horror and the flying things of night (like those eclipses in which the moon quite swallows up the sun and stands alone before it with a radiant ring)—this mode of thought and feeling, which Herder, the great delineator of the East, has so exactly painted for the North,[11] could but approach romantic poetry by the path by which a kindred Christianity quite reached and formed it.

We come at length to Christian romanticism, respecting which we must first show why in the South (particularly in Italy and Spain) it took on and created other forms than in the North, where, as was shown above, the very soil made of the heathen outer-court a romantically Christian

11 Above all in his *Alteste Urkunde* (Riga, 1774), p. 95, and *Zerstreute Blätter*, IV (Gotha, 1792), 131.

Holy of Holies. In its natural environment, and then because of manifold historic connections, the South presents an aspect so very different from the North that such reflections as derive romanticism from sources wholly distinct from Christian ones must be considered or corrected.

For the southerly and earliest variety, Bouterwek names these sources: [12] first, the heightened respect for womankind, brought in by the ancient Goths, then, the more spiritualized form of love.

But it was the Christian temple that gave shelter to romantic love, not the prehistoric German forest, and a Petrarch who is not a Christian is unthinkable. The one and only Mary ennobles every woman; hence, while a Venus can only be beautiful, a Madonna can be romantic. This higher form of love was or is precisely a blossoming and blooming from out Christianity, which, with its consuming hatred of the earthly, transformed the beautiful body into the beautiful soul that one might love the other—beauty, then, in the infinite. The name "Platonic love" is borrowed, notoriously, from another sort of love, from that pure unsullied friendship between youths in itself so innocent that the Greek lawgivers counted it a duty, so fanatical that the lover was punished for the errors of the loved one; here, then, simply directed toward another sex, we have again as with the ancient Goths the same deifying love, held—to prevent its profanation—as far as possible from nature, not the love that sanctifies through Christianity and clothes the loved one with the luster of romance.

The spirit of chivalry—which, apart from this, embroidered side by side upon its banners love and religion, Dame and Notre Dame—and the Crusades, named sires of romanticism as second choices, these are children of the Christian spirit. . . . To enter the promised land, which two religions at once and the greatest being on earth had elevated for the imagination to a twilight realm of holy anticipation and to an isthmus between the first world and the second, to enter this land was to glorify oneself romantically and with two strengths, with valor and with faith, to make oneself master, literally and poetically, of one's baser earthly nature. What comparable result could the heroic ages and the voyages of the Argonauts bring forth?

As servants and silent creatures of romanticism we reckon further the ascending centuries which, allying all peoples more and more closely with one another, round off their sharp corners from without, while from within, through the rising sunlight of abstraction, like a form of Christianity, they break up more and more the solid material world. All this emboldens one to prophesy that, as time goes on, the writing of poetry

---

12 *Geschichte der Poesie und Beredsamkeit*, I, 22.

will become more and more romantic, freer from rules or richer in them, that its separation from Greece will become wider and wider, and that the wings of its winged steed will so multiply that, precisely with the crowd, it will experience greater and greater difficulty in maintaining a steady course, unless, like Ezekiel's seraphim, it uses certain wings merely to cover its face.[13] But as for that, what concern have aestheticians and their prolegomena with time and eternity? Is only creeping philosophy to make progress, and soaring poetry lamely to gather rust? After three or four thousand years and their millions of horae is there to be no other division of poetry than Schiller's dull division of it into the horae [14] of the sentimental and the naïve? One might maintain that every century is romantic in a different way, just as one might, in jest or in earnest, place a different sort of poetry in every planet. Poetry, like all that is divine in man, is fettered to its time and place; at one time it must become Carpenter's Son and Jew, yet at another its state of abasement may begin on Mount Tabor and its transfiguration take place on a sun and blind us.[15]

Aside from this, it follows of itself that Christianity, although the common father of all romantic children, must in the South beget one sort of child, in the North another. The romanticism of the South—in Italy, climatically related to Greece—must blow more gently in an Ariosto, flying and fleeing less from the antique form, than that of the North in a Shakespeare, just as in turn the same southern variety takes on a different and orientally bolder form in torrid Spain. The poetry and the romanticism of the North is an aeolian harp through which the tempest of reality sweeps in melodies, its howlings resolved in tones, yet melancholy trembles on these strings—at times indeed a grief rends its way in.

· · · · ·

---

13 Ezekiel, 1:11; Isaiah, 6:2.
14 Jean Paul is using the word "horae" (*Horen*) both in its literal sense and in reference to the periodical *Die Horen*, edited by Schiller and

published monthly from 1795 to 1797; see Note a above.
15 An ancient tradition makes Mount Tabor the scene of the Transfiguration.

2. W. H. Wackenroder

Born at Berlin in 1773, Wackenroder was one of the first of the German romanticists. He was a fellow student of Ludwig Tieck's at Erlangen and Göttingen and inspired his friend with his own enthusiasm for the art of the Middle Ages. Wackenroder sought with romantic fervor to penetrate the mystery of music and emphasized in his writings the close relationship between religious feeling and artistic creation. This is the main theme of his *Herzensergiessungen eines kunstliebenden Klosterbruders* (1797). Wackenroder's premature death at the age of twenty-five was a great blow to Tieck, who completed and published his friend's posthumous *Phantasien über die Kunst für Freunde der Kunst* (1799).

The Remarkable Musical Life of the Musician Joseph Berglinger [1]

[*From* Herzensergiessungen eines kunstliebenden Klosterbruders]

[*1797*]

I have often looked backward and gathered in for my enjoyment the art-historical treasures of past centuries; but now my inclination impels me to tarry for once with the present time and to try my hand at the story of an artist whom I knew from his early youth and who was my most intimate friend. Alas, to my regret you soon departed this world, my Joseph, and not easily shall I find your like again! But I shall console myself by retracing in my thoughts the story of your genius, from the beginning, and by retelling it for those to

<hr>

1 Text: *Kunstanschauung der Frühromantik,* ed. by Andreas Müller (Leipzig, 1931), 89–105.

10

whom it may give pleasure—just as, in happy hours, you often spoke of it to me at length, and just as I myself came inwardly to know you.

JOSEPH BERGLINGER was born in a little town in the south of Germany. His mother was taken from the world as she brought him into it; his father, already a somewhat elderly man, was a doctor of medical science in straitened circumstances. Fortune had turned her back on him, and it was only by dint of much perspiration that he got along in life with his six children (for Joseph had five sisters), the more so since he was now without a capable housekeeper.

The father had formerly been a tender and very kindhearted man who liked nothing better than to give such help, counsel, and alms as he could afford; after a good deed, he slept better than usual; deeply moved and grateful to God, he could long thrive on the good works of his heart; he nourished his spirit in preference with affecting sentiments. Indeed, one cannot but give way to a profoundly melancholy admiration when one contemplates the enviable simplicity of these souls who discover in the ordinary manifestations of a kindly heart a source of grandeur so inexhaustible that it becomes the whole heaven on earth that reconciles them to the world at large and preserves them in constant and comfortable contentment. When he considered his father, Joseph was entirely of this mind; but Heaven had once and for all so constituted him that he aspired steadily to something higher; he was not content with mere spiritual health or satisfied that his soul should carry out its ordinary earthly tasks —to work and to do good; he wanted it to dance as well in exuberant high spirits—to shout to Heaven, as to its source, for joy.

His father's temperament, however, comprised still other elements. He was a hard-working and conscientious doctor and had known no other diversion, his whole life long, than the curious knowledge of things hidden in the human body and the vast science of all the wretched ills and ailments of mankind. As often happens, this intensive study became a secret enervating poison which penetrated his very artery and gnawed, in his breast, through many a responsive cord. To this was added his discontent with his wretched poverty, and finally his age. All these things served to undermine his former kindliness, for, where the soul is not strong, whatever a man comes into contact with is absorbed into his blood and alters his inner nature without his knowing it.

The children of the old doctor grew up under his care like weeds in a deserted garden. Joseph's sisters were some of them sickly, some of them feeble-minded, and, in their dark little room, they led a pitiable and lonely life.

In such a family no one could have been more out of place than Joseph, whose whole life was a beautiful fantasy and a heavenly dream. His soul was like a delicate young tree whose seed a bird has dropped into a ruined wall, where, among the rough stones, it springs up like a maiden. He was always by himself, alone and quiet, feeding only on his inner fantasies; on this account, his father considered him too a little foolish and unbalanced. He was sincerely fond of his father and his sisters, but most of all he prized his inner life, keeping it secret and hidden from others. Thus one secretes a jewel casket, to which one gives no one the key.

Music had from the first been his chief joy. Occasionally he heard someone play the piano and could even play a little himself. In time, by means of this often-repeated pleasure, he developed himself in a way so peculiarly his own that his being became thoroughly musical and his temperament, lured on by the art, wandered about continually among the shady bypaths of poetic feeling.

An outstanding chapter in his life was a visit to the episcopal residence, whither a well-to-do relation, who lived there and had taken a fancy to him, carried him off for a few weeks. Here he was really in his element; his spirit was fascinated by beautiful music, thousand-sided, and, not unlike a butterfly, it fluttered about in the congenial breeze.

Above all he visited the churches to hear the sacred oratorios, cantilenas, and choruses resounding in the full blast of trumpet and trombone beneath the vaulted roofs; from inner piety, he often listened humbly on his knees. Before the music began, as he stood there in the tightly packed and faintly murmuring congestion of the crowd, it seemed to him as though he heard buzzing about him, unmelodiously confused, as at a great fair, the commonplace and ordinary life of man; his brain was paralyzed with empty earthly trivialities. Full of expectation, he awaited the first sound of the instruments; as this now broke forth from out the muffled silence, long drawn and mighty as the sigh of a wind from heaven, and as the full force of the sound swept by above his head, it seemed to him as though his soul had all at once unfurled great wings—he felt himself raised up above the barren heath, the dark cloud-curtain shutting out the mortal eye was drawn, and he soared up into the radiant sky. Then he held his body still and motionless, fixing his gaze steadfastly on the floor. The present sank away before him; his being was cleansed of all the pettiness of this world—veritable dust on the soul's luster; the music set his nerves tingling with a gentle thrill, calling up changing images before him with its changes. Thus, listening to certain joyous and soul-stirring songs in praise of God, he seemed quite plainly to see David in his royal mantle, a crown upon his head, dancing toward him and shouting psalms before the Ark of the Covenant; he saw all his enthusiasm, all his movements, and his heart leapt in his breast. A thousand sensations latent within him were liberated and marvelously interwoven. Indeed, at certain passages in the music, finally, an isolated ray of light fell on his soul; at this, it seemed to him as though he all at once grew wiser and was looking down, with clearer sight and a certain inspired and placid melancholy, on all the busy world below.

This much is certain—when the music was over and he left the church, he thought himself made purer and more noble. His entire being still glowed with the spiritual wine that had intoxicated him, and he saw all passersby with different eyes. Now, when he chanced to see a group of people standing together on the pavement and laughing or exchanging gossip, it made a quite peculiarly disagreeable impression on him. As long as you live, he thought, you must hold fast, unwavering, to this beautiful poetic ecstasy, and your whole life must be a piece of music. When he went to lunch at his relation's and had thoroughly enjoyed his meal in a company not more than usually hearty and jovial, it displeased him that he had let himself be drawn again so soon into the prosaic life and that his rapture had vanished like a gleaming cloud.

His whole life long he was tormented by this bitter dissension between his inborn lofty enthusiasm and our common mortal lot, which breaks in daily on our reveries, forcibly bringing us down to earth.

When Joseph was at a great concert he seated himself in a corner, without so much as glancing at the brilliant assembly of listeners, and listened with precisely the same reverence as if he had been in church—just as still and motionless, his eyes cast down to the floor in the same way. Not the slightest sound escaped him, and his keen attention left him in the end quite limp and exhausted. His soul, eternally in motion, was wholly a play of sounds; it was as though, liberated from his body, it fluttered about the more freely, or even as though his body too had become a part of his soul—thus freely and easily was his entire being wound round with the lovely harmonies, and the music's foldings and windings left their impress on his responsive soul. At the lighthearted and delightful symphonies for full orchestra of which he was particularly fond, it seemed to him quite often as though he saw a merry chorus of youths and maidens dancing on a sunny meadow, skipping forward and backward, single couples speaking to each other in pantomime from time to time, then losing themselves again amid the joyous crowd. Certain passages in this music were for him so clear and forceful that the sounds seemed words.

At other times again, the music called forth a wondrous blend of gladness and sadness in his heart, so that he was equally inclined to smile and weep—a mood we meet so often on our way through life, for whose expression there is no fitter art than music. And with what delight and astonishment he listened to that sort of music which, beginning like a brook with some cheery, sunny melody, turns imperceptibly and wonderfully, as it goes on, into increasingly troubled windings, to break at last into a loud and violent sob, or to rush by, as though through a wild chasm, with an alarming roar! These many-sided moods now all of them impressed upon his soul new thoughts and visual images, invariably corresponding—a wondrous gift of music, the art of which it may be said in general that the more dark and mysterious its language, the greater its power to affect us, the more general the uproar into which it throws all forces of our being.

The happy days that Joseph had spent in the episcopal residence came to an end at last, and he returned again to his birthplace and to his father's house. How sad was this return—how doleful and depressed he felt at being once more in a household whose entire life and strife turned only on the bare satisfying of the most essential physical needs and with a father who so little approved of his inclinations, who despised and detested all the arts as servants of extravagant desires and passions and as flatterers of the elegant world! From the very first it had displeased him that his Joseph had so fastened his heart on music; now that this inclination in the boy was growing by leaps and bounds, he made a determined and serious effort to convert him, from a harmful propensity for an art whose practice was little better than idleness and which catered merely to sensual excess, to medicine, as the most beneficent science and as the one most generally useful to the human race. He took great pains to instruct his son himself in its elementary principles and gave him books to read.

This was a truly distressing and painful situation for poor Joseph. Secretly he buried his enthusiasm deep in his breast, not to offend his father, and sought to compel himself, if possible, to master a useful science on the side. Yet in his soul there was a constant struggle. In his textbooks he could read one page ten times over without grasping what he read; unceasingly within, his soul sang its melodious fantasies on and on. His father was much distressed about him.

In secret his passionate love of music came to dominate him more and more. If for several weeks he heard no music, he became actually sick at heart; he noted that his feelings dried up, an emptiness arose within him, and he experienced a downright longing to be again inspired. Then even ordinary players, on church festival and consecration days, could with their wind instruments move him to feelings which they themselves had never felt. And as often as a great concert was to be heard in a neighboring town, he rushed out, ardent and eager, into the most violent snow, storm, or rain.

Scarcely a day went by without his calling sadly to mind those wonderful weeks in the episcopal residence, without his soul's reviewing the priceless things that he had heard there. Often he repeated to himself from memory the lovely and touching words of the sacred oratorio which had been the first that he had heard [2] and which had made a particularly deep impression on him:

> Stabat mater dolorosa
> Juxta crucem lacrymosa,
> > Dum pendebat Filius
> Cujus animam gementem,
> Contristantem et dolentem,
> > Pertransivit gladius.
>
> O quam tristis et afflicta
> Fuit illa benedicta
> > Mater Unigeniti!
> Quae moerebat, et dolebat,
> Et tremebat, cum videbat
> > Nati poenas inclyti.

And so forth.

But alas for those enchanted hours, in which he lived as in an ethereal dream or had just come quite intoxicated from the enjoyment of a splendid piece of music; when they were interrupted for him—by his sisters, quarreling over a new dress, by his father, unable to give the eldest daughter enough money for her housekeeping or telling the story of a thoroughly wretched and pitiable invalid, or by some old beggar-woman, all bent over, coming to the door, unable to shield herself in her rags from the wintry frost—alas, there is in all the world no feeling so intensely bitter and heart-rending as that with which Joseph was then torn. Dear God, he thought, is this the world as it is—and is it Thy will that I should plunge into the turmoil of the crowd and share the general misery? So it seems, and, as my father constantly preaches, it is the destiny and duty of man to share it, to give advice and alms, to bind up loathesome wounds, to heal odious diseases. And yet again an inner voice calls out to me quite clearly:

---

2 Wackenroder is probably thinking of the setting by Pergolesi.

"No! No! You have been born to a higher, nobler end!" With thoughts like these he often tormented himself for hours at a time, finding no way out; before he knew it, however, there vanished from his soul those unpleasant pictures which seemed to pull him by force into the mire of this life, and his spirit floated once more unruffled on the breeze.

In time he became thoroughly convinced that God had sent him into the world to become a really distinguished artist, and it may sometimes have occurred to him that, in view of the gloomy and confining poverty of his youth, Providence might be going to reward him all the more brilliantly. Many will consider it a novelesque and unnatural invention, but it is none the less strictly true that in his loneliness, from an ardent impulse of his heart, he often fell on his knees and prayed God to so guide him that he might some day become an altogether splendid artist in the sight of God and man. At this time, his pulse often violently agitated by the pressure of ideas directed steadily toward one point, he wrote down a number of shorter poems, setting forth his state of mind or the praise of music, and these, without knowing the rules, he set joyously to music after his childish heartfelt fashion. A sample of these songs is the following, a prayer which he addressed to music's sainted patron:

> See me comfortless and weeping,
> Solitary vigil keeping,
>   Saint Cecilia, blessed maid;
> See me all the world forsaking,
> On my knees entreaty making;
>   Oh, I pray thee, grant me aid.
>
>   .   .   .
>
> Let the hearts of men be captured,
> By my music's tones enraptured,
>   Till my power has no bound,
> And the world be penetrated,
> Fantasy-intoxicated,
>   By the sympathetic sound.

Perhaps for more than a year poor Joseph tormented himself, brooding alone over the step he wished to take. An irresistible force drew his spirit back to that splendid city which he regarded as his paradise, for he was consumed by the desire to learn his art there from the ground up. But it was his relations with his father that weighed particularly on his heart. Having no doubt observed that Joseph was no longer at all willing to apply himself seriously and industriously to his scientific studies, his father had indeed already half given him up, withdrawing himself into his displeasure which, with his advancing age, increased by leaps and bounds. He no longer paid much attention to the boy. Joseph, meanwhile, did not on this account give up his childlike feeling; he struggled continually against his inclination and still had not the heart to breathe, in his father's presence, a word of what he had to reveal. For whole days at a time he tortured himself by weighing one course against another, but he simply could not extricate himself from the horrible abyss of doubt; his ardent prayers were all to no avail—this almost broke his heart. To the utterly gloomy and distressed state of mind in which he was at this time, these lines, which I found among his papers, bear witness:

> Ah, what are these forces that surround me
> And in their embrace have tightly bound me,
> Calling me away—shall I obey them?
> Urging me from home—can I gainsay them?
> I must bear, though guiltless of transgression,
> Torture and temptation and oppression.
>
> .   .   .
>
> That Thou'lt deign to save me, I implore Thee
> Bury me in earth, call me before Thee;
> Otherwise I cannot long withstand it,
> Must live at the will (if it demand it)
> Of that unknown force whose awful power
> Governs me more fully every hour.

From day to day his distress grew more and more acute, the temptation to escape to the splendid city stronger and stronger. But, he thought, will not Providence come to my aid—will it give me no sign at all? His suffering finally reached its highest peak when his father, in connection with some family disagreement, addressed him sharply in a tone quite different from his usual one, afterwards consistently repulsing him. Now the die was cast; from now on he turned his back on all doubts and scruples; he would now consider the matter no further. The Easter holiday was at hand; this he would celebrate with the others at home; but as soon as it was over—out into the wide world.

It was over. He awaited the first fine morning, for the bright sunshine seemed to lure him on as though by magic; then, early in the morning, he ran out of the house and away—one was used to this in him—but this time he did not come back. With delight and with a pounding heart he hastened through the narrow alleys of the little town; hurrying past everything he saw about him, he could scarcely keep from leaping into the open air. On one corner he met an old relation. "Why in such a hurry, cousin?" she asked. "Are you fetching vegetables for the table from the market again?" Yes, yes, called Joseph to himself, and, trembling with joy, he ran out through the gates.

But when he had gone a little distance into the country, he looked about and burst into tears. Shall I turn back, he thought. But he ran on, as though his heels were on fire, and wept continually, so that it looked as though he were running away from his tears. His way led now through many an unfamiliar village and past many an unfamiliar face; the sight of the unfamiliar world revived his courage, he felt strong and free—he came nearer and nearer—and at last—Heavens, what delight! —at last he saw lying before him the towers of the splendid city.

PART TWO

I return to my Joseph a number of years after we left him; he has become Capellmeister in the episcopal residence and lives in great splendor. His relation, having received him very cordially, has been the author of his good fortune, has seen to it that he was given the most thorough training in music, and has also more or less reconciled Joseph's father, little by little, to the step his son had taken. By exceptional application Joseph has worked his way up, to attain at length the highest rung of success that he could possibly wish.

Yet the things of this world change before our very eyes. On one occasion, after he had been Capellmeister for several years, he wrote me the following letter:

DEAR PATER:

It is a miserable life I lead—the more you seek to comfort me, the more keenly I am aware of it.

When I recall the dreams of my youth—how blissfully happy I was in those dreams! I thought I wanted to give my fancy free rein continuously and to let out my full heart in works of art. But how strange and austere even my first years of study seemed to me—how I felt when I stepped behind the curtain! To think that all melodies (although they had aroused the most heterogeneous and often the most wondrous emotions in me) were based on a single inevitable mathematical law—that, instead of trying my wings, I had first to learn to climb around in the unwieldy framework and cage of artistic grammar! How I had to torture myself to produce a thing faultlessly correct with the machine-like reason of ordinary science before I could think of making my feelings a subject for music! It was a tiresome mechanical task. But even so, I still had buoyant youthful energy and confidence in the magnificent future. And now? The magnificent future has become the lamentable present.

What happy hours I spent as a boy in the great concert hall, sitting quietly and unnoticed in a corner, enchanted by all the splendor and magnificence, and wishing ever so ardently that these listeners might some day gather to hear my works, to surrender their feelings to me! Now I sit often enough in this same hall, even perform my works there, but in a very different frame of mind indeed. To think I could have imagined that these listeners, parading in gold and silk, had gathered to enjoy a work of art, to warm their hearts, to offer their feelings to the artist! If, even in the majestic cathedral, on the most sacred holiday, when everything great and beautiful that art and religion possess violently forces itself on them, these souls are not so much as warmed, is one to expect it in the concert hall? Feeling and understanding for art have gone out of fashion and become unseemly; to feel, in the presence of an artwork, is considered quite as odd and laughable as suddenly to speak in verse and rhyme in company, when one otherwise gets through one's life with sensible prose, intelligible to all. Yet for these souls I wear out my spirit and work myself up to do things in such a way that they may arouse feeling! This is the high calling to which I had believed myself born.

And when on occasion someone who has a sort of halfway feeling seeks to praise me and to commend me critically and to propound critical questions for me to answer, I am always tempted to beg him not to be at such pains to learn about feeling from books. Heaven knows, when I have enjoyed a piece of music—or any other delightful work of art—and my whole being is full of it, I should paint my feeling on the canvas with a single stroke, if only a single color could express it. I cannot bestow false praise, and I can bring forth nothing clever.

To be sure, there is a little consolation in the thought that perhaps—in some obscure corner of Germany to which this or that work of mine may penetrate some day, even though long after my death—there may be someone whom Heaven has made so sympathetic to my soul that he will feel on hearing my melodies precisely what I felt in writing them—precisely what I sought to put in them. A lovely idea, with which, no doubt, one may pleasantly deceive oneself for a time!

Most horrible of all, however, are those other circumstances with which the artist is hemmed in. To speak of all the loathsome envy and spiteful conduct, of all the untoward petty customs and usages, of all the subordination of art to the will of a court—to speak a word of this is repugnant to me; it is all so undignified, so humiliating to man's soul, that I cannot bring a syllable of it past my lips. A threefold misfortune for music that the mere existence of a work requires such a number of hands! I collect myself and lift up my entire soul to produce a great work—and a hundred unfeeling empty-headed fellows put in their word and demand this and that.

In my youth I thought to avoid the misery of earthly life; now, more than ever, I have sunk into the mire. This much seems certain, sad to say—for all our exertion of our spiritual wings we cannot escape this earth; it pulls us back by force, and we fall again into the common human herd.

They are pitiable artists, those I see about me, even the noblest ones so petty that, for conceit, they do not know what to do once a work of theirs has become a general favorite. Dear God, is not one half our merit due to art's divinity, to nature's eternal harmony, the other half to the gracious Creator who gave us the power to make use of this treasure? Those charming melodies which can call forth in us the most varied emotions thousandfold, have they not sprung, all of them, from the unique and wondrous triad, founded an eternity since by nature? Those melancholy feelings, half soothing, half painful, which music inspires in us, we know not how, what are they after all but the mysterious effect of alternating major and minor? Ought we not to thank our Maker if he now grants us just the skill to combine these sounds, in sympathy from the first with the human soul, so that they move the heart? Art, surely, is what we should worship, not the artist—he is but a feeble instrument.

You see that my ardor and my love for music are no less strong than formerly. And this is just the reason why I am so miserable in this . . . but I shall drop the subject and not annoy you further by describing all the loathsome reality about me. Enough—I live in a very impure atmosphere. How far more ideally I lived in those days when I still merely enjoyed art, in youthful innocence and peaceful solitude, than I do now that I practice it, in the dazzling glare of the world, surrounded only by silks, stars and crosses of honor, and people of culture and taste! What should I like? I should like to leave all this culture high and dry and run away to the simple shepherd in the Swiss mountains to play with him those Alpine songs which make him homesick wherever he hears them.

From this fragmentarily written letter one can realize in part the situation in which Joseph found himself. He felt neglected and alone amid the buzzing of the many unharmonious souls about him; his art was deeply degraded in his eyes in that, so far as he knew, there was no one on whom it made a lively impression, for it seemed to him created only to move the human heart. In many a dark hour he was in utter despair, thinking: How strange and singular is art! Is then its mysterious power for me alone—is it to all other men mere sensual pleasure and agreeable amusement? What is it really and in fact, if it is nothing to all men and something to me alone? Is it not a most absurd idea to make this art one's whole aim and chief business and to imagine a thousand wonderful things about its great effects on human temperament—about an art which, in everyday reality, plays much the same role as card-playing or any other pastime?

When such thoughts occurred to him, it seemed to him that he had been the greatest of visionaries to have striven so hard to make a practical artist of himself for the world. He hit on the idea that the artist should be artist for himself alone, to his own heart's exaltation, and for the one or two who understand him. And I cannot call this idea wholly incorrect.

But I must sum up briefly the remainder of my Joseph's life, for my memories of it are beginning to depress me.

For a number of years he continued to live on in this way as Capellmeister, and, as time went on, his discouragement increased, as did his uneasy realization that, for all his deep feeling and intimate understanding of art, he was of no use to the world, less influential than a common tradesman. Often and regretfully he recalled the pure ideal enthusiasm of his boyhood and with it how his father had tried to make a doctor of him so that he might lessen man's misery, heal the unfortunate, and thus make himself useful in the world. This had perhaps been better, he thought more than once.

His father, meanwhile, had at his age grown very weak. Joseph wrote regularly to his eldest sister and sent her something toward his father's support. He could not bring himself to pay him an actual visit and felt that this would be beyond him. He became more despondent; his life was far spent.

On one occasion he had performed in the concert hall a new and beautiful piece of music of his own composition; it seemed the first time that he had made any impression on the hearts of his listeners. The general astonishment, the silent approval, so much more welcome than noisy applause, made him happy in the thought that this time he had perhaps been worthy of his art; once more he was encouraged to begin work anew. But when he went out on to the street, a girl, dressed very miserably, crept up and sought to speak to him. Heavens, he cried; it was his youngest sister and she was in a wretched state. She had run on foot from her home to bring him the news that his father was about to die and had insistently demanded to speak with him before the end. At that, the music in his breast broke off; in a heavy stupor he made his preparations and set off in haste for his birthplace.

The scenes which took place at his father's bedside I shall not describe. But let the reader not believe that there were any melancholy long-drawn-out debates; without wasting many words they understood each other fully—in this respect, indeed, it seems that nature mocks us generally, men never understanding one another properly until these critical last moments. At the same time, he was smitten to the heart by all that he saw.

His sisters were in the most deplorable circumstances; two of them had fallen from grace and run away; the eldest, to whom he regularly sent money, had wasted most of it, letting his father starve; in the end his father died miserably before his eyes; alas, it was horrible, the way his poor heart was wounded through and through and torn to bits. He did what he could for his sisters and went home, for his affairs recalled him.

For the impending Easter festival he was to write a new passion music; his envious rivals were eagerly awaiting it. Yet, as often as he sat down to work, he burst into a flood of tears; his tortured heart would not let him recover himself. He lay deeply depressed, buried among the leavings of this world. At length, by an effort, he tore himself free, stretching out his arms to heaven in an impassioned prayer; he filled his soul with the most sublime poetry, with a full and exultant hymn, and, in a marvelous inspiration, but still violently shaken emotionally, he set down a passion music which, with its deeply affecting melodies, embodying all the pains of suffering, will forever remain a masterpiece. His soul was like that of the invalid who, in a strange paroxysm, exhibits greater strength than the healthy man.

But after he had performed the oratorio in the cathedral on Easter Sunday, straining himself to the utmost in feverish agitation, he felt faint and exhausted. Like an unhealthy dew, a nervous weakness attacked all his fibers; he was ill for a time and died not long afterwards, in the bloom of his years.

Many a tear have I offered to his memory, and a strange feeling comes over me when I review his life. Why did Heaven ordain that the struggle between his lofty enthusiasm and the common misery of this earth should make him unhappy his whole life long and in the end tear quite apart the twofold nature of his mind and body?

The ways of Providence are hidden from us. But let us marvel once again at the diversity of those inspired beings whom Heaven sends into the world to serve the arts.

A Raphael brought forth in all innocence and artlessness works of the utmost ingenuity in which we see revealed the whole of Heaven; a Guido Reni, leading a wild gambler's life, created the gentlest and most sacred paintings; an Albrecht Dürer, a simple citizen of Nuremberg, in that same cell in which his wicked wife abused him daily, produced with the antlike industry of the mechanic art-works highly spiritual in content; yet Joseph, in whose harmonious music lies such mysterious beauty, differed from them all.

Alas, his lofty fantasy was what destroyed him. Shall I say that he was perhaps created rather to enjoy art than to practice it? Are those in whom art works silently and secretly, like an inner genius, not hindering their doings upon earth, perhaps more fortunately constituted? And must the ceaselessly inspired one, if he would be true artist, perhaps not weave his lofty fantasies, like a stout strand, boldly and firmly into this earthly life? Indeed, is not perhaps this incomprehensible creative power something altogether different and—as it now seems to me—something still more marvelous and godlike than the power of fantasy?

The spirit of art is and remains for man eternally a mystery, and he grows dizzy when he seeks to plumb its depths; at the same time, it is eternally an object for his highest admiration, as must be said of all the great things in this world.

But after these recollections of my Joseph I can write no more. I conclude my book—in the hope that it may have served to awaken good ideas in some one or other of my readers.

3. Jean Paul

From the Hesperus [1]

[1795]

I. GARDEN CONCERT BY STAMITZ

I SHOULD not have allowed the hairdresser [2] to sing and carry on so long, had I been able to use my hero, this entire Sunday, for anything more than a figurant; but the whole day he did nothing of any account except that, out of charity perhaps, he obliged our old friend Appel—by himself unpacking her boxes and chests of drawers—to prepare, printed with typographical splendor, the regular Sabbath edition of her body, which preferred dressing hams to dressing itself, as early as three o'clock in the afternoon; ordinarily she did not deliver this till after supper. The Jews believe that on the Sabbath they get a new Sabbath soul; into girls there enters at least one; into Appel there entered at least two.

But why should I today expect more action from my hero—from him, who today—absorbed in his dream-night and in the coming evening— moved by each friendly eye and by the urns of the spring which he had dreamed away—gently dissolved by the peaceful tepid summer which lay smiling and dying on the incense-burning altars of the mountains, on the

1 Text: *Sämtliche Werke*, I. Abteilung, III (Weimar, 1929), 289-294. The scene is the garden of Chamberlain Le Baut in St. Lüne, an imaginary watering-place not far from Flachsenfingen, the capital of a likewise imaginary principality; the supposed date is Sunday, October 21, 1792. Chamberlain Le Baut has arranged a garden concert in honor of the birthday of his daughter Clothilde. Besides Clothilde, the assembled company includes Pastor Peter Eyman and his wife, their daughters Agathe and Apollonia (Appel), Chamberlain Le Baut and his second wife, and Victor (also called by his middle name, Sebastian), the hero of the novel, supposedly the heir of Lord Horion, an English peer, but actually the son of Pastor Eyman. Jean Paul admits

that Victor is to some extent a self-portrait. Throughout the evening Victor is under the spell of a dream which had come to him the night before: in this he stands beneath the evening star upon a plain covered with forget-me-nots and encircled by pyramids of ice, tinted by the setting sun; Clothilde appears to him, deathlike and serene, led by winged children; flower-covered funeral mounds are seen to rise and fall; into these mounds Clothilde sinks to the heart; forget-me-nots cover her; butterflies, doves, and swans with outspread wings cling to the purple peaks; at the summit of the highest peak he sees Clothilde again, transfigured, her arms outstretched.

2 Meuseler, the local wig-maker, a member of the village choir.

meadows draped in muslin, and beneath the receding funeral procession of the birds, now hushed, and which, as the first cloud rose against the foliage, departed—from Victor, I repeat, who today, smiled upon sadly by one tender recollection after another, felt that till now he had been far too merry. He could only look upon the good souls about him with loving, shimmering eyes, turn these away again still more shimmering and say nothing and go out. Over his heart and over his every note stood the word *tremolando*. No one is more deeply sad than he who smiles too much; for if once this smiling stops, then anything has power over the compliant soul, and a foolish lullaby, a flute concerto—whose d- and f-sharp keys and embouchures are but two lips with which a shepherd boy is piping—sets free the well-remembered tears as a slight sound the threatening avalanche. It seemed to him as though the morning's dream did not at all allow him to address Clothilde; she seemed to him too sacred, still led on by winged children and seated by them on thrones of ice. Because today he simply had no tongue or ears for Le Baut's conversations in the realm of the morally dead, he would listen unobserved in the great leafy garden to Stamitz's concert [3] and, at the most, allow himself to be presented by chance. His second reason was his heart, created as a sounding board for music; by preference this absorbed the fleeting sounds undisturbed, hiding their effects from ordinary men, who in truth can no more do without the works of Goethe, Raphael, and Sacchini (and for no less important reasons) than without those of Löschenkohl.[4] It is true that emotion lifts us above the shame of showing emotion; but in his emotional moments he shunned and hated all attention to the attentions of others, for the devil smuggles vanity into the best of feelings, one often knows not how. In the night, in the shadow, tears fall more easily and evaporate more slowly.

The parson's wife encouraged him in everything; for she had secretly —sent to town, invited her son,[5] and trumped up a surprise in the garden.

At length the parson's family elevated itself to the leafy concert hall, little knowing how much they were looked down on by the family Le Baut, who accepted only noble metals and noble birth as tickets of admis-

---

3 In August 1792, Carl Stamitz played in concert at Hof, where Jean Paul lived during the writing of the *Hesperus* (see Hans Bach's introduction to Vol. 3 of the *Sämtliche Werke*, p. xxxiv).

4 Johann Löschenkohl, Viennese engraver and art dealer. "His things were thrown on the market with the utmost haste, yet despite their faulty drawing and coloring—time did not permit better workmanship—people actually fought over them. Of his engraving 'Maria Theresia on Her Death Bed,' 7,000 copies at two gulden each were sold within a few days. With his restless industrial activity he produced without tiring and was always offering something new—silhouettes, portraits in miniature, calendars; he opened a factory for the manufacture of boxes, of fans, of buttons, and was responsible for setting many fashions" [Wurzbach, *Biographisches Lexikon des Kaiserthums Oesterreich*].

5 Flamin, actually the illegitimate son of the local prince and of Le Baut's first wife, Clothilde's mother.

sion and who rated the parson's family highly as friends of milord [6] and Matthieu,[7] but would have rated them still more highly as their lap dogs.

Victor remained behind a moment in the garden of the parsonage, because it was still too light, also because he felt sorry for poor Apollonia; the latter, in gala attire, lonely and unobserved, was gazing out into space from the window of the little garden house and rocking his godchild [8] straight up and down, holding him now above her head, now below her waist. Like a small-town worthy Victor kept on his hat in the garden house, hoping to stimulate her courage by politeness. The child in arms is, as it were, the prompter and bellows treader of the nursemaid; the young Sebastian lent Appel sufficient reinforcement against the old one, and at length she ventured to speak and to observe that the godchild was a dear, good, beautiful "Bastel." "But," she added, "the *gnädige Frölen* (Clothilde) mustn't hear me say so; she wants us to call him Victor when she hears Father say 'Bastel.' " Then she made much of how Clothilde loved his godchild, of how she took the little rascal from her and smiled at him and kissed him; and everything she praised the panegyrist repeated with the little one. Nay, even the grown-up Sebastian imitated it, but on the tiny lips he sought only another's kisses; and perhaps in Appel's case his own were among the things for which she sought. A happier man took leave of a happier woman; for Cupid now sent one bright hope after another to his heart as messengers and every one bore the same message: "We do not belie thee, truly; have faith in us!"

At last Stamitz began to tune, a thing the grand-chamberlain's tenacious purse would certainly not have bothered about, since there were today no strangers present, if Clothilde had not asked to have this garden concert as the sole celebration of her birth night. Stamitz and his orchestra filled a lighted arbor—the noble auditorium sat in the nearest, most brightly lighted niche and wished it were already over—the common one sat further off and the chaplain, afraid of the catarrhal dewy floor, twined one leg around the other over the thigh—Clothilde and her Agathe rested in the darkest leafy box. Victor did not steal in until the overture announced to him the seat and the sitting of the company; in the furthest arbor, at the true aphelion, this comet found a place. The overture consisted of that musical scratching and scrawling—of that harmonious phraseology —of that firework-like crackling of passages sounding one against another —that I so highly recommend, if it is only in the overture. There it belongs; it is the fine rain that softens the heart for the bigger drops of the

---

6 Lord Horion.
7 Matthieu von Schleunes, son of the prince's Minister.

8 Sebastian, the Eymans' youngest child.

simpler sounds. Every emotion requires its exordium; and music clears the way for music—or for tears.

Stamitz climbed gradually—following a dramatic plan not drawn up by every capellmeister—from the ears into the heart, as though from Allegros into Adagios; this great composer sweeps in narrower and narrower circles about the breast that holds a heart until he finally reaches it and in ecstasy embraces it.

Without seeing his beloved, Horion trembled alone in the dark arbor into which a single dried-up branch let in the light of the moon and of its driving clouds. Nothing ever moved him more, while listening to music, than to watch the clouds course by. When, with his eyes and with the music, he followed these nebulous streams in their eternal flight about our shadow orb, when he relinquished to them all his joys and his desires; then, as in all his joys and sorrows, he thought of other clouds, of another flight, of other shadows than those above him, then his whole soul longed and yearned; but the music stilled the longing as the bullet in the mouth stills thirst, and harmony loosed the flooding tears from his full soul.

Faithful Victor! in man there is a great desire, never fulfilled; it has no name, it seeks no object, it is nothing that you call it nor any joy; but it returns, when on a summer's night you look toward the north or toward the distant mountains, or when there is moonlight on the earth, or when the heavens are bright with stars, or when you are very happy. This great monstrous desire exalts our spirit, but with sorrows: Alas, prostrate here below, we are hurled into the air like epileptics. But this desire, to which nothing can give a name, our songs and harmonies name it to the human spirit—the longing spirit then weeps the more vehemently and can control itself no longer and calls amid the music in sobbing rapture: Truly, all that you name, I lack.

The enigmatic mortal likewise has a nameless, monstrous fear that has no object, that is awakened when one hears ghostly apparitions, and that is sometimes felt when one but speaks of it. . . .

With silent tears whose flowing no one saw, Horion abandoned his battered heart to the lofty Adagios, which spread themselves with warm eider-down wings over all his wounds. All that he loved came now into his shadow-arbor, his oldest and his youngest friend—he hears the raging of life's thunderstorms, but the hands of friendship reach out to one another and clasp and in the second life they still hold one another incorrupt.

Each note seemed a celestial echo of his dream, answering to beings whom one did not see and did not hear. . . .

He could not possibly stay longer in this dark enclosure with his burning fantasies and at this too great distance from the pianissimo. He approached the music—almost too boldly and too closely—through a leafy corridor, leaning far forward through the foliage in order at last to see Clothilde in the distant green shimmer. . . .

Ah, he did see her! But too lovely, too celestial! He saw, not the pensive eye, the cold mouth, the tranquil form that forbade so much and desired so little; for the first time he saw her mouth enveloped by a sweet harmonious pain in an indescribably touching smile—for the first time he saw her eyes weighed down under a great tear, like forget-me-nots bent under a tear of rain. Oh, this kind creature indeed concealed her finest feelings most of all! But the first tear in a beloved eye is too much for an overly tender heart. . . . Victor knelt down, overpowered by reverence and bliss, before the noble soul and lost himself in the shadowy weeping figure and in the weeping sounds. And then, when he saw her features grow pale, for the green foliage cast upon her lips and cheeks a deathlike reflection from the lanterns—and when his dream appeared again and in it the Clothilde who had sunk beneath the flowery mound— and when his soul dissolved in dreams, in sorrows, in joys, and in desires for the creature who was consecrating her birthday feast with pious tears, then was it still necessary to his dissolution that the violin ceased sounding and that the second harmonica, the *viole d'amour*, sent forth its sphere harmonics to his naked, inflamed, and throbbing heart? Oh, the aching of this bliss appeased him, and he thanked the creator of this melodic Eden for having relieved his bosom, his sighs, and his tears with the harmonica's highest notes, which with an unknown force split into tears the heart of man, as high notes burst a glass; amid such sounds, after such sounds, there was no further place for words; the full soul was enshrouded by leaves and night and tears—the swelling speechless heart absorbed the tones unto itself and took the outer tones for inner ones—and at the end the tones played only softly, like zephyrs, about his listless rapture, and only within his expiring inner self did there still falter the overly blissful wish: "Alas, Clothilde, if only I might today give up to you this mute and glowing heart—alas, if only I might, on this memorable heavenly evening, sink dying at your feet with this trembling soul and speak the words, 'I love thee!'"

And when he thought of her festival, and of her letter to Maienthal,[9]

---

[9] In this letter to her tutor, Clothilde had written: "Today in the garden I thought of your Maienthal with a longing that was almost too sad; Herr Sebastian often reminds me of it, for he appears to have had a teacher much like my own." Victor now knows that Clothilde's tutor Emanuel and his own tutor Dahore are one and the same.

which had paid him the high compliment of calling him Emanuel's pupil, and of little signs of her respect for him, and of the beautiful companionship of his heart and hers—then amid the music there came to him vividly and for the first time the bright hope of winning this ennobled heart, and with this hope the harmonica tones flowed like radiating echoes far over the whole future of his life. . . .

. . . . .

2. FRANZ KOCH'S DOUBLE MOUTH-HARMONICA [10]

I jumped to my feet at the name Franz Koch.[11] If one of my readers is a guest at Carlsbad for the waters, or His Majesty King William II of Prussia, or a member of his court, or the Elector of Saxony, or the Duke of Brunswick, or some other princely personage, he will have heard the excellent Koch, a modest soldier on half pay who travels about everywhere, playing his instrument. This last, which he calls "double mouth-harmonica," consists in an improved pair of simultaneously played Jew's harps, which he exchanges after every piece of music. His way of playing the Jew's harp compares with the old way as do the bells of musical glasses with a servant's bell. It is my duty to persuade those of my readers whose imaginations have wren's wings, or who are lithopaedic (stillborn), at least from the heart out, or who have eardrums only to drum on, to persuade such readers, with what few oratorical powers I have, to throw the said Franz out of doors if he should come and offer to hum before them. For there is nothing to him, and the most miserable viola or straw-fiddle screams, in my opinion, more shrilly; indeed, his music is so delicate that in Carlsbad he never strikes up before more than twelve customers at one time, it being impossible to sit close enough to him, and when he plays his best pieces he actually has the light carried out so that neither eye nor ear may disturb the fantasy. But should one reader be otherwise disposed—a poet, perhaps—or a lover—or very delicate—or like Victor—

---

10 Text: *ibid.,* IV (Weimar, 1929), 52–58. The scene is the house of Chamberlain Le Baut; the supposed date is Tuesday, April 2, 1793.

11 "Franz (Paul) Koch, celebrated German virtuoso on the Jew's harp, was born in 1761 at Mittersill near Salzburg and as a boy learned the book-binding trade. In 1782 recruiting officers induced the itinerant worker to come to Magdeburg, where he was at once pressed into service as a grenadier. In this capacity an officer chanced to hear him play his Jew's harp (mouth harmonica) and spoke to others of his amazement at Koch's skill, so that the soldier's reputation soon spread even as far as Berlin and Potsdam. King Friedrich Wilhelm II sent for Koch, listened to him play, and ordered him discharged from his involuntary service in the army. Encouraged from every quarter, Koch now went on tour and attracted uncommon attention, so that even Jean Paul (in his *Hesperus*) took note of him. The year of his death is not known. A more detailed account of his life appears in Schummel's almanac for 1793 (p. 322)" [Mendel, *Musikalisches Conversations-Lexikon*]. Like Stamitz, Koch played in concert at Hof in August 1794.

or like myself, then let him hearken unhesitatingly, his soul at peace and ready to melt, to Franz Koch—or—since at this precise moment he is not to be had—to me.

My witty English friend [12] had sent this harmonist to Victor with a card: "The bearer is the bearer of an echo which he keeps in his pocket." Victor, on this account, preferred to take him over to Clothilde, the friend of all musical beauty, in order that her departure might not deprive her of this hour of melody. He felt as though he were going down a long aisle in a church when he entered Clothilde's Santa Casa; her simple room, like Our Lady's, was enclosed within a temple. She had already finished her black finery. A black costume is a lovely darkening of the sun, in the midst of which one cannot take one's eyes off it. Victor, who with his Sinese awe of this color brought to this magic a defenseless soul, a kindled eye, grew pale and confused at Clothilde's sympathetic features, over which the trace of a recently fallen rain of sorrow hovered like a rainbow against a bright blue sky. Hers was not the serenity of diversion—which every girl derives from dressing herself—it was the serenity of a pious soul filled with love and patience. He was embarrassed at having to walk among thistles of two sorts—the painted ones on the parquet, on which he was continually stepping, and the satiric ones of the nice observers about him, against which he was continually pricking himself. Her stepmother [13] was still busied with the plastering and painting of her body corruptible, and the evangelist [14] was in her dressing room as toilet acolyte and collaborator. Hence Clothilde had still time to hear the mouth-harmonist; and the chamberlain offered himself to his daughter and to our hero—for he was a father who knew what to do where his daughter was concerned—as a part of the audience, although he could make little of music, dinner music and dance music excepted.

Not until now did Victor gather, from Clothilde's joy over the musician he had brought with him, that her harmonious heart vibrated gladly to music; altogether, he was often wrong about her because she—like you, dearest ————, expressed with silence both her highest praise and highest blame. She asked her father, who had heard the mouth-harmonica before in Carlsbad, to give her and Victor an idea of it—he gave one: "It expresses in masterly fashion both the fortissimo and the piano-dolce and, like the single harmonica, it lends itself most readily to the Adagio." To this she replied—on Victor's arm, which was guiding her to a quiet room, darkened for the music—"Music is perhaps too good for drinking songs

---

12 "Cato the Elder," an illegitimate son of the local prince

13 Le Baut's second wife.
14 Matthieu von Schleunes.

and for the expression of merriment. Just as suffering ennobles a man, unfolding him by the little pricks it gives him as regularly as one splits open with a knife the bud of a carnation that it may bloom with bursting, so music, as a sort of artificial suffering, takes the place of the genuine variety." "Is genuine suffering so unusual?" Victor asked, in the darkened room, lighted only by a single wax candle. He sat down next to Clothilde, and her father seated himself opposite them.

Blissful hour that thou once broughtest to my soul with the echoing music of thy harmonica—speed by once more, and may the reverberations of that echo again sound about thee!

Scarcely had the modest quiet virtuoso laid the implement of enchantment to his lips than Victor felt that (while the light still shone) he might not, as he usually did, paint scenes of his own to each Adagio and adapt to each piece particular inspirations from his poems. For an infallible means of giving music the omnipotence that belongs to it is to make of it an accompaniment to one's own inner melody, turning instrumental music into vocal, as it were, inarticulate sounds into articulate ones, not permitting the lovely succession of tones, to which no definite object lends alphabet or language, to glide from our hearts, leaving them bathed but not made tender. Hence, when the loveliest sounds that ever flowed from human lips as consonants (or consonances) of the soul began to flutter from the trembling mouth-harmonica; when he felt that these tiny rings of steel, as though the frame and fingerboard of his heart, would make their convulsions his; he forced his feverish heart, whose every wound bled afresh today, apart from the music, to contract itself against it and to paint itself no pictures, merely so that he might not burst into tears before the light was taken away.

Higher and higher rose the dragnet of uplifting tones, carrying his captive heart aloft. One melancholy reminiscence after another, in this spectral hour of the past, called out to him: "Do not suppress me, give me my tear." All his pent-up tears collected about his heart, and his whole inner self, lifted off the bottom, swam gently in them. Yet he composed himself: "Canst thou not yet deny thyself (he asked), not even a moistened eye? No, with a dry eye receive this muffled echo of thy whole breast, receive this Arcadian resonance and all these tearful sounds into your distraught soul." In the midst of this veiled distillation, which he often took for fortitude, it always seemed to him as though there were addressing him, from distant parts, a breaking voice whose words had the rhythm of verse; once again the breaking voice addressed him: "Are not these tones composed of faded hopes? Do not these sounds run one into another, Horion, like the days of man? O look not on thy heart! There, as it turns to dust, the shimmering days of yore have etched themselves as in a mist!" Nevertheless he replied, still quietly: "Life is after all too short for the two tears—for the tear of woe and for the other." . . . But now—as the white dove that Emanuel saw falling in the cemetery [15] sped through the images of his recollection—as he thought: "In my dream of Clothilde this dove was already fluttering and clinging to the iceberg; alas, it is the image of the fading angel beside me!"—as the music fluttered more and more quietly and at length stole back and forth among the whispering foliage of a funeral wreath—and as the breaking voice returned and said: "Dost not recall the familiar sounds? Lo, before her birthday feast they were already in thy dreams and there they lowered to the heart into the grave the sick soul beside thee, and she left thee but an eye filled with tears, a soul filled with grief!"—"No, more than that she did not leave me," his weary heart repeated haltingly, and all the tears he had held back came rushing to his eyes in streams. . . .

But, since the light had just been carried from the room, the first stream fell unnoticed into the lap of night.

The harmonica began the melody of the dead—"Wie sie so sanft ruhn." [16] Alas, in sounds like these the spent waves of the sea of eternity beat against the hearts of the somber watchers standing on the shore and yearning to put forth! Now, Horion, shalt thou be wafted by a sounding breeze out of the rainy mist of life into the clear hereafter. What sounds are these that fill the far-off fields of Eden? Do they not hark back, dissipated as breath, to distant flowers and flow, swollen by the echo, about the swanlike breast that, blissfully expiring, swims on pinions and draw it from melodic tide to tide and sink with it into the distant flowers that a mist of perfumes fills, and, in the dark perfume, does not the soul catch fire like a sunset before it blissfully departs?

Ah, Horion, does the earth still rest beneath us that bears its funeral mounds around the breadth of life? Is it in earthly air that these sounds vibrate? O Music, thou who bringest past and future so near our wounds with their flying flames, art thou the evening breeze from this life or the morning air of the life to come? In truth, thine accents are echoes, gath-

---

15 A reference to an earlier letter in which Emanuel gives an account of a conversation between himself and the blind Julius, Lord Horion's son, and foretells the circumstances of his own death. " 'Now a white dove flies over the deep blue like a great dazzling snowflake . . . Now it circles about the sparkling golden tip of the lightening-rod, as though about a glimmering star hung in the sunlit sky—it weaves and weaves and sinks and disappears among the tall flowers of the cemetery . . . Julius, didst thou feel nothing as I spoke? Alas, the white dove was perhaps thy angel [Clothilde]; perhaps this is why thy heart dissolved today at its approach" (ibid., III, 400).

16 "The Cemetery" (Der Gottesacker), words by A. C. Stockmann, music by Pastor F. B. Beneken (1787); cf. Max Friedländer, Das deutsche Lied im 18. Jahrhundert (Stuttgart, 1902), I, 318; II, 130; Musikbeispiel 181.

ered by angels from the joyous sounds of a second world to bring to our
mute hearts, to our deserted night, the faded spring song of the soaring
heavens! And thou, re-echoing sound of the harmonica, thou comest to
us truly from a shout that, ringing from heaven to heaven, dies out at
last in that remotest, stillest heaven of them all, consisting only of a deep,
broad, eternally silent rapture. . . .

"Eternally silent rapture," repeated Horion's melted soul, whose delight I have in the foregoing made my own, "yes, there the country lies,
there where I lift up mine eyes to the all-benevolent and hold out my arms
to her, to this weary soul, to this great heart—then, Clothilde, will I fall
on my heart, then will I cling to thee forever, and the flood of that
eternally silent rapture shall envelop us. Breathe once again toward life,
ye earthly tones, between my breast and hers, then let there float toward
me over your clear waves a tiny night, an undulating silhouette, and I
will look on it and say: 'This was my life'—then will I say more softly,
weeping more intensely: 'Indeed, man is unhappy, but only on the
earth.' "

Oh, if there be a mortal over whom, at these last words, memory draws
great rain clouds, then I say to him: Beloved brother, beloved sister, I
am today as touched as thou, I respect the grief thou hidest—ah, thou
forgivest me and I thee. . . .

The song stopped and died away. How silent now the darkness! All
sighing was clothed in halting breath. Only the nebulous stars of feeling
sparkled brightly through the gloom. No one could see whose eyes had
wept. Victor gazed into the still black air before him, which a few moments
earlier had been filled with hanging gardens of sound, ebbing air castles
of the human ear, miniature heavens, and which remained there as a
naked, blackened scaffolding for fireworks.

But the harmonica soon filled this gloom again with a mirage of other
worlds. Ah, why did it have to hit precisely on "Vergissmeinnicht," the
melody that gnawed at Victor's heart,[17] repeating the lines to him as
though he were himself repeating them to Clothilde: "Forget me not,
now that relentless fate calls thee from me—Forget me not, if loose and
cooling earth engulf this heart that gently beat for thee—Think it is I,
if echo answers in thy soul: 'Forget me not.' " . . . Oh, if after this these
sounds entwine themselves in waving flowers, flow back from one past
time into another, run more and more softly through the departed years

---

17 Words by Franz von Knebel, music by
Lorenz Schneider (1792); cf. Friedländer, *op. cit.*,
II, 448. Schneider's music was at first generally
attributed to Mozart and repeatedly published under his name (cf., Köchel, Anhang 246). In the
continuation of our first excerpt (omitted above),
Victor and Clothilde had heard the melody played
by Stamitz.

that lie behind mankind—finally murmur beneath the morning dawn of life—roll on unheard below the cradle of mankind—grow cold in our chill twilight and dry up in the midnight where no one of us has been; then, deeply moved, man ceases to conceal his sighs and his unending sorrows.

The silent angel beside Victor could no longer veil them, and Victor heard Clothilde's first sigh.

Then he took her by the hand, as though to support her, hovering, above an open grave.

She let him keep it, and her pulse beat tremulously in unison with his.

At length the last note of the song projected its melodious circles in the ether and flowed expanding over all past time—then a distant echo wrapped it in a fluttering breeze and wafted it through deeper echoes to that last echo lying round about the heavens—then the sound expired and sped as a soul into Clothilde's sigh.

At this, her first tear fell, like a burning heart, on Victor's hand.

•   •   •   •   •

4. E. T. A. Hoffmann

A standard-bearer of German romanticism, Hoffmann was born in 1776 at Königsberg and died in 1822 at Berlin. His talents were manifold: he was a poet, a critic, a composer, a theater manager, a draftsman, and a public servant. Best remembered for his fantastic novels, Hoffmann was deeply devoted to music and for some time made music his profession. Among his works for the stage the most important is the opera *Undine* (1813–1814). Hoffmann was one of the fathers of modern musical journalism and in this field opened the way to Schumann and Wagner. His literary works testify to the deeply musical nature of his poetic inspiration. In turn, Hoffmann's poetic visions have inspired musical works of the most disparate character. Schumann's *Kreisleriana*, Offenbach's *Les Contes d'Hoffmann*, Busoni's *Die Brautwahl* are cases in point.

Beethoven's Instrumental Music [1]

[1813]

WHEN WE speak of music as an independent art, should we not always restrict our meaning to instrumental music, which, scorning every aid, every admixture of another art (the art of poetry), gives pure expression to music's specific nature, recognizable in this form alone? It is the most romantic of all the arts—one might almost say, the only genuinely romantic one—for its sole subject is the infinite. The lyre of Orpheus opened the portals of Orcus—music discloses to man an unknown realm, a world that has nothing in common with the external sensual world that surrounds

---

[1] Text: *Sämtliche Werke*, ed. by C. G. von Maassen, I (Munich & Leipzig, 1908), 55–58, 60–61, 62–64. As published in 1814 among the "Kreisleriana" of the *Fantasiestücke in Callot's Manier* (and earlier, anonymously, in the *Zeitung für die elegante Welt* for December 1813), this essay combines and condenses two reviews published anonymously in the *Allgemeine musikalische Zeitung* (Leipzig) for July 1810 and March 1813.

him, a world in which he leaves behind him all definite feelings to surrender himself to an inexpressible longing.

Have you even so much as suspected this specific nature, you miserable composers of instrumental music, you who have laboriously strained yourselves to represent definite emotions, even definite events? How can it ever have occurred to you to treat after the fashion of the plastic arts the art diametrically opposed to plastic? Your sunrises, your tempests, your *Batailles des trois Empereurs*,[2] and the rest, these, after all, were surely quite laughable aberrations, and they have been punished as they well deserved by being wholly forgotten.

In song, where poetry, by means of words, suggests definite emotions, the magic power of music acts as does the wondrous elixir of the wise, a few drops of which make any drink more palatable and more lordly. Every passion—love, hatred, anger, despair, and so forth, just as the opera gives them to us—is clothed by music with the purple luster of romanticism, and even what we have undergone in life guides us out of life into the realm of the infinite.

As strong as this is music's magic, and, growing stronger and stronger, it had to break each chain that bound it to another art.

That gifted composers have raised instrumental music to its present high estate is due, we may be sure, less to the more readily handled means of expression (the greater perfection of the instruments, the greater virtuosity of the players) than to the more profound, more intimate recognition of music's specific nature.

Mozart and Haydn, the creators of our present instrumental music, were the first to show us the art in its full glory; the man who then looked on it with all his love and penetrated its innermost being is—Beethoven! The instrumental compositions of these three masters breathe a similar romantic spirit—this is due to their similar intimate understanding of the specific nature of the art; in the character of their compositions there is none the less a marked difference.

In Haydn's writing there prevails the expression of a serene and child-like personality. His symphonies lead us into vast green woodlands, into a merry, gaily colored throng of happy mortals. Youths and maidens float past in a circling dance; laughing children, peering out from behind the trees, from behind the rose bushes, pelt one another playfully with flowers. A life of love, of bliss like that before the Fall, of eternal youth; no sorrow, no suffering, only a sweet melancholy yearning for the beloved object

---

2 Perhaps Hoffmann is thinking of Louis Jadin's "La grande bataille d'Austerlitz," published in an arrangement for the piano by Kühnel of Leipzig in 1807 or earlier.

that floats along, far away, in the glow of the sunset and comes no nearer and does not disappear—nor does night fall while it is there, for it is itself the sunset in which hill and valley are aglow.

Mozart leads us into the heart of the spirit realm. Fear takes us in its grasp, but without torturing us, so that it is more an intimation of the infinite. Love and melancholy call to us with lovely spirit voices; night comes on with a bright purple luster, and with inexpressible longing we follow those figures which, waving us familiarly into their train, soar through the clouds in eternal dances of the spheres.[a]

Thus Beethoven's instrumental music opens up to us also the realm of the monstrous and the immeasurable. Burning flashes of light shoot through the deep night of this realm, and we become aware of giant shadows that surge back and forth, driving us into narrower and narrower confines until they destroy *us*—but not the pain of that endless longing in which each joy that has climbed aloft in jubilant song sinks back and is swallowed up, and it is only in this pain, which consumes love, hope, and happiness but does not destroy them, which seeks to burst our breasts with a many-voiced consonance of all the passions, that we live on, enchanted beholders of the supernatural!

Romantic taste is rare, romantic talent still rarer, and this is doubtless why there are so few to strike that lyre whose sound discloses the wondrous realm of the romantic.

Haydn grasps romantically what is human in human life; he is more commensurable, more comprehensible for the majority.

Mozart calls rather for the superhuman, the wondrous element that abides in inner being.

Beethoven's music sets in motion the lever of fear, of awe, of horror, of suffering, and wakens just that infinite longing which is the essence of romanticism. He is accordingly a completely romantic composer, and is not this perhaps the reason why he has less success with vocal music, which excludes the character of indefinite longing, merely representing emotions defined by words as emotions experienced in the realm of the infinite?

The musical rabble is oppressed by Beethoven's powerful genius; it seeks in vain to oppose it. But knowing critics, looking about them with a superior air, assure us that we may take their word for it as men of great intellect and deep insight that, while the excellent Beethoven can scarcely be denied a very fertile and lively imagination, he does not know how to bridle it! Thus, they say, he no longer bothers at all to select or to shape his ideas, but, following the so-called daemonic method, he dashes every-

---

a Mozart's Symphony in E-flat major, known as the "Swan Song."

thing off exactly as his ardently active imagination dictates it to him. Yet how does the matter stand if it is *your* feeble observation alone that the deep inner continuity of Beethoven's every composition eludes? If it is *your* fault alone that you do not understand the master's language as the initiated understand it, that the portals of the innermost sanctuary remain closed to you? The truth is that, as regards self-possession, Beethoven stands quite on a par with Haydn and Mozart and that, separating his ego from the inner realm of harmony, he rules over it as an absolute monarch. In Shakespeare, our knights of the aesthetic measuring-rod have often bewailed the utter lack of inner unity and inner continuity, although for those who look more deeply there springs forth, issuing from a single bud, a beautiful tree, with leaves, flowers, and fruit; thus, with Beethoven, it is only after a searching investigation of his instrumental music that the high self-possession inseparable from true genius and nourished by the study of the art stands revealed.

Can there be any work of Beethoven's that confirms all this to a higher degree than his indescribably profound, magnificent symphony in C minor? How this wonderful composition, in a climax that climbs on and on, leads the listener imperiously forward into the spirit world of the infinite! . . . No doubt the whole rushes like an ingenious rhapsody past many a man, but the soul of each thoughtful listener is assuredly stirred, deeply and intimately, by a feeling that is none other than that unutterable portentous longing, and until the final chord—indeed, even in the moments that follow it—he will be powerless to step out of that wondrous spirit realm where grief and joy embrace him in the form of sound. The internal structure of the movements, their execution, their instrumentation, the way in which they follow one another—everything contributes to a single end; above all, it is the intimate interrelationship among the themes that engenders that unity which alone has the power to hold the listener firmly in a single mood. This relationship is sometimes clear to the listener when he overhears it in the connecting of two movements or discovers it in the fundamental bass they have in common; a deeper relationship which does not reveal itself in this way speaks at other times only from mind to mind, and it is precisely this relationship that prevails between sections of the two Allegros and the Minuet and which imperiously proclaims the self-possession of the master's genius.

How deeply thy magnificent compositions for the piano have impressed themselves upon my soul, thou sublime master; how shallow and insignificant now all seems to me that is not thine, or by the gifted Mozart or that mighty genius, Sebastian Bach! With what joy I received thy seventieth work, the two glorious trios, for I knew full well that after a little practice I should soon hear them in truly splendid style. And in truth, this evening things went so well with me that even now, like a man who wanders in the mazes of a fantastic park, woven about with all manner of exotic trees and plants and marvelous flowers, and who is drawn further and further in, I am powerless to find my way out of the marvelous turns and windings of thy trios. The lovely siren voices of these movements of thine, resplendent in their many-hued variety, lure me on and on. The gifted lady who indeed honored me, Capellmeister Kreisler,[3] by playing today the first trio in such splendid style, the gifted lady before whose piano I still sit and write, has made me realize quite clearly that only what the mind produces calls for respect and that all else is out of place.

Just now I have repeated at the piano from memory certain striking transitions from the two trios.

. . . . . .

How well the master has understood the specific character of the instrument and fostered it in the way best suited to it!

A simple but fruitful theme, songlike, susceptible to the most varied contrapuntal treatments, curtailments, and so forth, forms the basis of each movement; all remaining subsidiary themes and figures are intimately related to the main idea in such a way that the details all interweave, arranging themselves among the instruments in highest unity. Such is the structure of the whole, yet in this artful structure there alternate in restless flight the most marvelous pictures in which joy and grief, melancholy and ecstasy, come side by side or intermingled to the fore. Strange figures begin a merry dance, now floating off into a point of light, now splitting apart, flashing and sparkling, evading and pursuing one another in various combinations, and at the center of the spirit realm thus disclosed the intoxicated soul gives ear to the unfamiliar language and understands the most mysterious premonitions that have stirred it.

That composer alone has truly mastered the secrets of harmony who knows how, by their means, to work upon the human soul; for him, numerical proportions, which to the dull grammarian are no more than cold, lifeless problems in arithmetic, become magical compounds from which to conjure up a magic world.

Despite the good nature that prevails, especially in the first trio, not even excepting the melancholy Largo, Beethoven's genius is in the last

---

3 The eccentric, half-mad musician from whose literary remains Hoffmann pretends to have taken his "Kreisleriana." Schumann borrows the title of his Opus 16 from these sketches of Hoffmann's (published in two groups as a part of his *Fantasiestücke in Callot's Manier*).

analysis serious and solemn. It is as though the master thought that, in speaking of deep mysterious things—even when the spirit, intimately familiar with them, feels itself joyously and gladly uplifted—one may not use an ordinary language, only a sublime and glorious one; the dance of the priests of Isis can be only an exultant hymn. Where instrumental music is to produce its effect simply through itself as music and is by no means to serve a definite dramatic purpose, it must avoid all trivial facetiousness, all frivolous *lazzi*. A deep temperament seeks, for the intimations of that joy which, an import from an unknown land, more glorious and more beautiful than here in our constricted world, enkindles an inner, blissful life within our breasts, a higher expression than can be given to it by mere words, proper only to our circumscribed earthly air. This seriousness, in all of Beethoven's works for instruments and for the piano, is in itself enough to forbid all those breakneck passages up and down for the two hands which fill our piano music in the latest style, all the queer leaps, the farcical capriccios, the notes towering high above the staff on their five- and six-line scaffolds.

On the side of mere digital dexterity, Beethoven's compositions for the piano really present no special difficulty, for every player must be presumed to have in his fingers the few runs, triplet figures, and whatever else is called for; nevertheless, their performance is on the whole quite difficult. Many a so-called virtuoso condemns this music, objecting that it is "very difficult" and into the bargain "very ungrateful."

Now, as regards difficulty, the correct and fitting performance of a work of Beethoven's asks nothing more than that one should understand him, that one should enter deeply into his being, that—conscious of one's own consecration—one should boldly dare to step into the circle of the magical phenomena that his powerful spell has evoked. He who is not conscious of this consecration, who regards sacred Music as a mere game, as a mere entertainment for an idle hour, as a momentary stimulus for dull ears, or as a means of self-ostentation—let him leave Beethoven's music alone. Only to such a man, moreover, does the objection "most ungrateful" apply. The true artist lives only in the work that he has understood as the composer meant it and that he then performs. He is above putting his own personality forward in any way, and all his endeavors are directed toward a single end—that all the wonderful enchanting pictures and apparitions that the composer has sealed into his work with magic power may be called into active life, shining in a thousand colors, and that they may surround mankind in luminous sparkling circles and, enkindling its imagination, its innermost soul, may bear it in rapid flight into the faraway spirit realm of sound.[4]

---

[4] Hoffmann's essay was brought to Beethoven's attention in February or March 1820 by someone who wrote, during a conversation with him: "In the *Fantasiestücke* of Hoffmann there is much talk about you. Hoffmann used to be the music-director in Bromberg; now he is a state counsellor. They give operas by him in Berlin." On the strength of this, evidently, Beethoven wrote the following letter to Hoffmann on March 23, 1820:

Through Herr ——, I seize this opportunity of approaching a man of your intellectual attainments. You have even written about my humble self, and our Herr —— showed me in his album some lines of yours about me. I must assume, then, that you take a certain interest in me. Permit me to say that, from a man like yourself, gifted with such distinguished qualities, this is very gratifying to me. I wish you the best of everything and remain, sir,

Your devoted and respectful
Beethoven.

5. E. T. A. Hoffmann

The Poet and the Composer [1]
[1819–1821]

[From Die Serapions-Brüder]

THE ENEMY was at the gates, cannons thundered all about, and grenades, spouting fire, cut whistling through the air. The citizens, their faces pale with fear, ran to their lodgings, and the empty streets echoed with the clattering hoofs of the cavalry patrols, charging hither and yon, cursing and driving from the rear those soldiers who had been left behind. Only Ludwig sat in his back room, completely immersed in the magnificent, varicolored world that his fancy had revealed to him before the piano; he had just finished a symphony in which he had endeavored to fix in black and white all the music of his innermost self, a work which, like Beethoven's compositions in this vein, was to speak in god-like language of the sublime wonders of that faraway romantic land in which we live perishing in inexpressible yearning; indeed, which was itself, like one of those wonders, to enter into our narrow, needy life and to entice out of it, with a lovely siren song, those willingly surrendering to it. Just then his landlady came into the room, reproaching him that in the midst of the general distress and emergency he could only play the piano and asking him whether he wanted to be shot to death there in his attic room. Ludwig really did not understand the woman until at that moment a grenade, roaring by, tore away a piece of the roof and broke in the windowpanes with a clatter; then the landlady ran screaming and howling down the stairs to the cellar with Ludwig hastening after her, carrying under his arm his most precious possession, the score of his symphony. Here the entire company of the house was assembled. In an attack of generosity otherwise by no means characteristic, the innkeeper who lived on the ground floor had sacrificed a couple of dozen bottles of his best wine; the women, trembling, hesitant, but as usual mindful of the needs and nourishment of the body, had brought in knitting-baskets many a dainty morsel from their

1 Text: *Sämtliche Werke*, ed. by C. G. von Maassen. The *Serapions-Brüder*, a collection of short tales set in the framework of a connecting narrative, is named for a little group of friends who meet once a week to exchange stories. The original members of this "club" are Lothar, Theodor (a composer), Ottmar, and Cyprian; the present story is told by Theodor.

kitchen surplus; one ate, one drank, one was soon transported from a state exalted by fear and anxiety to that sociable, comfortable state in which one neighbor, pressing himself against another, seeks security and thinks he has found it, and in which, as it were, that mincing, formal dance step which convention teaches is swallowed up in the great waltz to which the bronze fist of destiny beats time. Forgotten was the precarious situation, even the apparent mortal danger, and lively scraps of conversation poured from eager lips. Inmates of the house who, meeting one another on the stairs, scarcely touched their hats, sat side by side, hand in hand, revealing their innermost selves in hearty, mutual interest. The shots fell more sparingly, and some were already speaking of going upstairs, since the street seemed to be becoming safe. An old veteran went further and, after obliging by way of introduction with a few instructive words on the art of fortification among the ancient Romans and on the effect of catapults and, from more modern times, touching approvingly on Vauban, was on the point of demonstrating that fear was entirely uncalled for, since the house lay quite beyond the line of fire, when a bullet, striking the bricks that shielded the ventilator, hurled them into the cellar. No one was hurt, however, and when the old soldier sprang, glass in hand, upon the table, from off which the bricks had knocked the bottles, and defied the absent bullet, all took courage anew.

This, incidentally, was the last alarm; the night passed quietly, and the next morning one learned that the army had occupied a new position, voluntarily evacuating the city to the enemy. While one was leaving the cellar, hostile troops were already roaming through the town, and a public notice promised the inhabitants peace and security of possession. Ludwig threw himself into the motley crowd which, curious as to the new drama, was going to meet the approaching hostile general, who presently rode through the gate, heralded by the merry calls of trumpets and surrounded by brilliantly dressed guards.

Scarcely could Ludwig believe his eyes when, among the adjutants, he caught sight of Ferdinand, his dearly beloved academic friend, who, wearing a plain uniform and carrying his left arm in a sling, curvetted by quite close to him on a magnificent dun horse. "It is he—it is truly, surely he himself!" Ludwig called out involuntarily. Having vainly sought to follow his friend, whose flying steed had carried him quickly away, Ludwig thoughtfully hurried back to his room; but no work would move from the spot; the appearance of his old friend, whom he had entirely lost sight of for years, filled his thoughts, and as though in a bright glow there came back to him that blissful youth which he and the sociable Ferdinand had wasted together. In those days Ferdinand had not shown the slightest inclination toward the military life; he had lived solely for his muse, and many a gifted piece of writing had borne witness to his poetic vocation. For this reason, his friend's transformation was the less understandable to Ludwig, who burned with desire to talk with him without knowing how to set about looking for him.

Now the place became more and more lively, a large division of the hostile troops passed by, and at their head rode the allied princes, who were granting themselves at this point a few days of rest. But the greater the turmoil became at main headquarters, the less hope Ludwig retained of seeing his friend again, until at length, in an out-of-the-way, little-patronized café where he was in the habit of taking his frugal supper, his friend, with a loud cry of the utmost joy, fell unexpectedly into his arms. Ludwig remained silent, for a certain disquieting feeling had made the longed-for moment of reunion a bitter one. He felt as one sometimes does in a dream when one embraces loved ones only to have them at once strangely change themselves, keenest joys giving way in an instant to mocking illusions.

The gentle son of the muse, the poet of many a romantic stanza which Ludwig then had clothed with harmony, stood before him in his high, plumed helmet, his heavy, clanking saber at his side, denying even his own voice, calling out in a harsh, rough tone. Ludwig's gloomy gaze fell on Ferdinand's wounded arm and from that passed upward to the medal of honor which he wore at his breast. Then Ferdinand embraced him with his right arm, pressing him violently and passionately to his breast.

(FERDINAND) I know what it is that you are thinking, what it is that you feel at this reunion!

The Fatherland called, and I dared not hesitate to answer. With the joy, with the burning enthusiasm which a sacred cause kindles in every breast that cowardice does not brand a slave's, this hand, otherwise used only to the quill, grasped the sword! I have shed my blood, and only the chance which brought it about that I did my duty under the eyes of the prince, won me this medal. But believe me, Ludwig, those lyre strings which have so often sounded within me, whose tones have so often spoken to you, are still unharmed; indeed, after horrible and bloody battling, on my lonely post, while the horsemen lay in the bivouac about the watchfire, I wrote with high enthusiasm many a song that uplifted and strengthened me in my glorious calling, the defense of honor and freedom.

At these words, Ludwig's inner hostility gave way; and, when Ferdinand had stepped with him into a private room and had laid aside helmet and saber, it seemed to him as though his friend had merely tried his patience with a strange disguise that he had now thrown off. Now, while the two friends consumed the modest repast that had been brought in to them in the meantime, and while their glasses clinked merrily one against another, a joyous mood came over them, the good old days, with all their bright lights and colors, surrounded them, and all those bewitching fancies which their common artistic urge had as it were conjured up with powerful spell returned once more in the resplendent brilliance of their renewed youth. Ferdinand inquired incidentally as to what Ludwig had composed in the meanwhile and was most astonished when the latter confessed to him that he had still not yet managed to write an opera and have it produced on the stage, since thus far, in subject matter and execution, no poem had proved at all capable of stirring him to composition.

(F) Why you have not long since written a libretto for yourself, I cannot understand, for you have an adequate command of language and, with your unusually lively imagination, you ought surely not to be at a loss for subject matter.

(LUDWIG) My imagination, I will admit, may well be lively enough for the invention of many a good subject; especially at night, when a light headache puts me into that dreamy condition that is as it were a battle between waking and sleeping, not only do right good, genuinely romantic operas indeed occur to me, but these are actually performed before me with my own music. Yet, as concerns the gift of retaining such things and writing them down, I believe I lack it; and after all, you can scarcely ask us composers, in order that we may write our own verses, to acquire that mechanical technique, essential to success in any art and attainable only by constant application and steady practice. But even if I had the knack of turning an invented theme correctly and with taste into scenes and verses, it is not likely that I would decide to write myself a libretto.

(F) Yet no one, after all, can enter into your musical tendencies as you can yourself.

(L) That is doubtless true; at the same time it would seem to me that the composer who sits down to the task of turning an invented opera subject into verse must be affected very much as a painter would be, if, before being allowed to begin his painting in live colors, he were first obliged to make a meticulous engraving of the image his imagination had conceived.

(F) You think that the fire needed for composing would burn itself out and be smothered in the work of versification?

(L) Actually, that is it! And in the end even my verses would seem to me miserable things, like the paper wrappers of the rockets which only yesterday were crackling through the air in fiery life. Seriously, though, it seems to me that, for the success of a work, it is in no art as necessary as it is in music to conceive the whole, with all its parts, down to the smallest detail, in the first and liveliest glow of inspiration; since nowhere is filing and altering more useless and more harmful, and also since I know from experience that the melody first brought to life, as though by magic, right while reading a poem, is always the best, perhaps indeed, from the composer's viewpoint, the only true one. It would be quite impossible for the composer not to busy himself, even while writing his poem, with the music which the situation called forth. Quite transported and working only on the melodies flooding toward him, he would search in vain for words, and, should he succeed in forcing himself to it, that stream, however powerfully its great waves might roar along, would all too soon run dry on the sterile sands. Indeed, to express my inner conviction still more forcefully, in the instant of musical inspiration all words—all phrases—would strike him as inadequate—insipid—contemptible, and he would have to climb down from his height to be able to beg in the lower region of words for the means of his existence. But would not his wings soon be lamed here, like those of the captive eagle, and would he not attempt in vain the flight to the sun?

(F) That, to be sure, is quite reasonable; but do you know, my friend, that you are not so much convincing me as excusing your unwillingness to first clear the way for musical creation with all the necessary scenes, arias, duets, etc.?

(L) That may be; but I shall renew an old complaint by asking why it was that, when a common artistic urge bound us together closely, you would never give in to my ardent wish that you should write a libretto for me.

(F) Because it seemed to me the world's most thankless task.

You will grant me that no one could be more self-centered in his requirements than you composers are; and if you maintain that I ought not to ask a musician to acquire the technique essential to the mechanical work of versification, then I shall on the other hand insist that for a poet to concern himself so exactly with your needs, with the structure of your trios, quartets, finales, etc., would add so much to his burden that he would, as indeed happens only too often, sin at every moment against the form which you have somehow adopted—with what justification I trust you know yourselves. And if, extending ourselves to the utmost, we have sought to fix each situation of our drama in genuine poesy and to depict it in the most inspired language and in perfectly rounded verses, then the way you often mercilessly cut out our finest lines and often mistreat our grandest phrases, turning them in the wrong way, inverting them, even drowning them in melody, is truly horrible.

I say this only of the vain task of working the poem out carefully. But even as to subject, many a magnificent one that has come to us as poetic inspiration and which we have brought to you, proud in the belief that we were conferring a great favor, you have refused point-blank as insignificant and unworthy of musical treatment. This, after all, is often mere conceit, or whatever you please to call it, for often you set your hands to texts that are beneath contempt, and . . .

(L) Stop, my good friend!

To be sure, there are composers to whom music is as foreign as poetry is to many a verse-carpenter; these, then, have often set music to texts that actually are in every respect beneath contempt. Genuine composers, living in and from their sublime and sacred art, choose only poetic texts.

(F) But Mozart . . . ?

(L) . . . chose in his classical operas only poems genuinely suited to music, paradoxical as this may seem.

But, putting this question aside for the moment, I believe it possible to specify quite precisely what sort of subject is suited to opera, so that a poet may never be in danger of erring in this.

(F) I confess that I have never reflected on it, and, in view of my want of musical knowledge, I should also have lacked the necessary premises.

(L) If by musical knowledge you mean the so-called theory of music, you will not need it to judge correctly of a composer's wants; for without it you can have so grasped the nature of music and so made it a part of you that, from this point of view, you may be a far better musician than one who, having in the sweat of his brow worked through the whole theory of music in all its labyrinthine detail, worships the dead letter, like a fetish he has carved himself, as the living spirit, and whom this idol-worship bars from the joys of a higher realm.

(F) And you believe that, without the school's having admitted him to those lower orders, the poet may penetrate the true nature of music?

(L) I do.

Indeed, in that faraway country, which surrounds us often with the strangest presentiments and from which wondrous voices call down to us, wakening all the echoes that sleep in our restricted breasts, which echoes, awakened now, shoot joyfully and gladly up, as though in fiery rays, making us sharers in the bliss of that paradise, there poets and musicians are members of a faith, related in the most intimate way; for the secret of word and tone is one and the same, and has admitted them to highest orders.

(F) I hear my dear Ludwig endeavoring to grasp, in deep parables, the mysterious nature of art; and, in truth, I already see the gap diminishing which formerly I thought divided the poet from the musician.

(L) Let me attempt to express my idea of the true nature of opera. In a word, it would seem to me that only that opera in which the music arises directly from the poem as its inevitable offspring is a genuine opera.

(F) I will confess that I do not yet quite follow you.

(L) Is not music the mysterious language of a faraway spirit world whose wondrous accents, echoing within us, awaken us to a higher, more intensive life? All the passions battle with one another, their armor shimmering and sparkling, perishing in an inexpressible yearning which fills our breasts. Such is the indescribable effect of instrumental music. Now, however, music is to come fully to life, is to take hold of life's phenomena and, beautifying word and deed, to speak of particular passions and situations. Can one then speak of the commonplace in elevated language? Can music then reveal anything to us beyond the marvels of that country from out which it calls?

Let the poet prepare himself for a bold flight into the faraway land of romance; there he will find the marvel that he is to bring to life, alive and gleaming with fresh color, so that one willingly believes in it, so indeed that one wanders as in a blissful dream among the flowery paths of romantic life, superior to the needs of everyday existence, so that one understands only the language of romance, words becoming sounding music.

(F) You would preserve, then, only the romantic opera, with its fairies, spirits, marvels, and transformations?

(L) Of course I regard the romantic opera as the only genuine one, for only in the land of romance is music at home. At the same time, you are, I dare say, ready to believe that I thoroughly despise those poverty-stricken medleys in which childish, spiritless spirits are conjured up and in which without regard for cause or effect marvel is piled on marvel, merely to flatter the eye of the indolent crowd. A genuinely romantic opera is written only by a gifted and inspired poet, for only such a one can bring to life the wondrous phenomena of the spirit world; on his wings we are lifted over the chasm which otherwise divides us from it, and, grown accustomed to the strange country, we believe in the marvels which, as inevitable effects of the action of higher natures on our being, take place visibly and bring about all the strong, powerfully affecting situations which fill us, now with awe and horror, now with the highest bliss. It is, in a word, the magic force of poetic truth which the poet representing the marvelous must have at his command, for only this can transport us; and a mere capricious succession of aimless fairy pranks which, as is usual in medleys of this kind, are only there to harass Pagliasso in his knight's costume, will, as farcical and stupid, leave us always cold and uninterested.

So, my friend, in an opera the action of higher natures on our being must take place visibly, thus opening up before our eyes a romantic exist-

ence in which language, too, is raised to a higher power, or rather, is borrowed from that faraway country—from music, that is, from song—where
action and situation themselves, vibrating in powerful harmonies, take
hold of us and transport us the more forcefully.

(F) Now I understand you fully, and I think of Ariosto and Tasso;
yet it will, I think, be difficult to form the musical drama to your specifications.

(L) This is the task of the gifted, genuinely romantic poet.

Think of the incomparable Gozzi. In his dramatized fairytales he has
succeeded perfectly in what I ask of a librettist, and it is incredible that
this rich vein of operatic subjects has not thus far been more exploited.

(F) I confess that Gozzi, when I read him some years ago, appealed
to me in the most lively fashion, although my point of view was naturally
a different one from that which you have adopted.

(L) One of his finest tales is undoubtedly that of the raven.[2]

. . . . .

(F) Now I recall the splendid, fantastic piece quite exactly and still
feel the deep impression that it made on me. You are right; here the
marvelous seems to be necessary, and it is poetically so true that one willingly believes in it. It is Millo's deed, the murder of the raven, which as
it were knocks at the gates of the gloomy spirit realm; now they open
sonorously, and the spirits stalk into life, ensnaring mankind in the wondrous, mysterious destiny that governs them.

(L) Quite so; and now consider the strong, splendid situations which
the poet knew how to spin out of this conflict with the spirit world. Jen-
naro's heroic self-sacrifice, Armilla's heroic deed—in these things lies a
grandeur of which our moralizing playwrights, burrowing into the miser-
ies of everyday life as though among the sweepings thrown from the
state hall into the dust cart, have no idea at all. How magnificently, too,
the comic characters of the masks are woven in!

(F) Yes indeed!

Only in the genuinely romantic do the comic and tragic combine so naturally that they blend as one in the total effect, laying hold of the feelings
of the audience in a wonderful way of their own.

(L) This even our opera hacks have dimly perceived. For hence, pre-

2 *Il Corvo*, "Fiaba teatrale tragicomica," first
performed in Venice on October 24, 1761. An
opera on this subject, by the Danish composer
J. P. E. Hartmann, was performed for the first
time in Copenhagen on October 29, 1832; Schumann has a long account of it in his *Gesammelte
Schriften*, III, 247–255. Another tale of Gozzi's
supplied Richard Wagner with the subject of
Die Feen.

sumably, have arisen the so-called heroic-comic operas in which so often it is the heroic that is really comic, while the comic is heroic only insofar as it heroically rides rough-shod over everything that taste, decency, and good morals require.

(F) According to the specification which you have laid down for the opera libretto, we have very few genuine operas indeed.

(L) Quite so!

Most of our so-called operas are only stupid plays with music, and the utter lack of dramatic effect which is blamed, now on the libretto, now on the music, is to be attributed to the dead weight of scenes strung together without inner poetic connection, without poetic truth, to which music could not give the spark of life. Often the composer has unconsciously worked quite for himself, and the miserable libretto runs alongside, unable to make any contact with the music. Then the music can in a certain sense be quite good, that is, without inner depth, without forcibly laying hold of the audience as though by magic, it can arouse a certain feeling of comfort, like a joyous, brilliant play of colors. Such an opera is a concert, given on a stage with costumes and scenery.

(F) Inasmuch as you are in this way admitting only the romantic opera, in the strictest sense of the word, how about the musical tragedies, and finally, the comic operas in modern costume? Must you discard these altogether?

(L) By no means!

In most of the older, tragic operas, such as are unfortunately no longer being written and composed, it is again the genuinely heroic in the action, the inner strength of characters and situations, which lays hold of the beholder so powerfully. The mysterious and somber force that governs gods and men stalks visibly before his eyes, and he hears revealed in strange, foreboding tones the eternal, unalterable decisions of fate which even rule the gods. From these purely tragic subjects the fantastic proper is excluded; but in the connection with the gods, who have awakened men to higher life, indeed to godlike deeds, there must be heard, in music's wondrous accents, a more elevated language. Incidentally, were not the antique tragedies already musically declaimed? And does this not right clearly argue the need for a higher means of expression than that which ordinary speech affords?

In a way all their own, our musical tragedies have inspired gifted composers to a sublime, shall I say, sacred style, and it is as though man were drifting, in a miraculous ecstasy, on sounds from the golden harps of cherubim and seraphim, into the realm of light, where is revealed to him the mystery of his own being.

I wished, Ferdinand, to suggest nothing less than the intimate relation of church music to tragic opera, from which the older composers formed a magnificent style of their own, of which the moderns—not excepting Spontini, boiling over in luxuriant abundance—have no idea. The incomparable Gluck, standing there like a hero, I prefer not to mention at all; but to perceive how even lesser talents have grasped that genuinely grand and tragic style, think of the chorus of the priests of Night, in Piccinni's *Didon*.

(F) Now I feel as I did in the earlier, golden days of our life together; in speaking inspiringly of your art, you lift me up to views otherwise beyond my range; and you may believe that at the moment I imagine that I understand a good deal about music.

Indeed, I believe that no good line can form itself within me except it come forth as music.

(L) Is this not the true enthusiasm of the librettist?

I maintain that he must from the first set everything to music inwardly, just as the musician does; and that only the clear consciousness of particular melodies, even of particular sounds of the instruments taking part, in a word, the ready control over the inner realm of sound, distinguishes the one from the other. But I still owe my opinion of the *opera buffa*.

(F) You will scarcely admit this, least of all in modern costume?

(L) For my part, I confess, dear Ferdinand, not only that, precisely in the costume of our time, it is most congenial to me, but that it seems true to me in this guise alone, true to its character, true to the intention of the animated, excitable Italians who created it. Here it turns now on the fantastic, which arises, in part from the reckless abandon of single characters, in part from the bizarre play of chance, and which impudently forces its way into everyday life, turning everything upside down. One has to admit: "Yes, it is Master Neighbor in his familiar, cinnamon-colored, Sunday suit with its buttons of spun gold; what in the world can have happened to the man to make him behave so foolishly?"

Imagine a respectable company of cousins and aunts with a languishing daughter; add to these some students, who sing to the cousin's eyes and play the guitar beneath her window. To these enters Hobgoblin Droll with a tantalizing spell, and in the ensuing confusion all is movement, and we have absurd fancies, strange pranks of every description, and outlandish contortions. A special star has risen, and everywhere chance stretches nets in which the most respectable people are caught, if they poke out their noses ever so little.

Precisely in this intrusion of the adventurous into everyday life, and in the contradictions arising from it, lies in my opinion the nature of the true *opera buffa;* and it is precisely this grasp of the otherwise remote fantastic, now entered into life, that makes the acting of the Italian comedians so inimitable. They understand the poet's implications, and their acting brings to life the skeleton, which is all that he could give, in flesh and color.

(F) I think I have understood you perfectly.

You believe, then, that in the *opera buffa* it is essentially the fantastic that replaces the romantic, your indispensable requirement of opera, and the poet's art consists for you in this: that he brings his characters on the stage, not only perfectly rounded and poetically true, but taken straight from everyday life and so individual that one at once says to oneself: "Look! There is the neighbor I talk with every day! There is the student who goes to class every morning and sighs so terribly beneath the cousin's window, etc.!" And now the reckless action, which they set in motion as though suffering from some strange delirium, or of which they are the victims, affects us, you think, as surprisingly as though a crazy hobgoblin were to go through life, irresistibly driving us all into the charmed circle of his laughable mischief-making.

(L) You express my idea exactly, and I need scarcely add how now, according to my principle, music readily accommodates itself to the *opera buffa,* and how here too a special style arises of itself which in its own way lays hold of the temper of the audience.

(F) But has music the power to express the comic in all its nuances?

(L) Of this I am thoroughly convinced, and gifted artists have demonstrated it hundreds of times. So, for example, there may lie in music the expression of the most entertaining irony, like that which predominates in Mozart's incomparable *Cosi fan tutte.*

(F) Here you force on me the comment that, according to your principle, the despised libretto of this opera is in reality genuinely operatic.

(L) Just this is what I had in mind when I maintained before that Mozart in his classical operas chose only poems genuinely suited to music, for all that the *Marriage of Figaro* is more of a play with music than a true opera. The fruitless attempt to transplant the tearful type of play into the opera house can only miscarry, and our "orphan asylums," [3] "eye

---

3 *Das Waisenhaus,* comic opera by Joseph Weigl (1808); Hoffmann reviewed this for the *Allge-* *meine musikalische Zeitung* (Leipzig) in September 1810.

doctors," [4] etc., will surely be forgotten soon. Nothing can be more contemptible and foreign to true opera than that whole series of *Singspiele*, like those Dittersdorf turned out,[5] though I energetically defend such operas as the *Sonntagskind* and the *Schwestern von Prag*.[6] They may be called real German *opere buffe*.

(F) These operas, at least, when well performed, have always entertained me thoroughly, and what goes straight to my heart is what Tieck has the poet say to the audience in the *Gestiefelter Kater*:[7] "If this is to entertain you, you must put aside whatever culture you have and actually become children, to enjoy and entertain yourselves as children do."

(L) Unfortunately these words, like many others of their kind, fell on hard, sterile soil, where they could not penetrate and take root. But the *vox populi*, as a rule an outright *vox Dei* in affairs of the theater, drowned out the individual sighs which superfine natures gave vent to, horrified at the lack of naturalness and taste exhibited in these—to their minds, childish—pieces, and there is reason to believe that, as though carried away by the folly that had laid hold of the common people, many a superior person, in the midst of his dignified behavior, broke into a shocking laugh, at the same time protesting that he could not understand his own laughter.

(F) Ought not Tieck to be the poet who, if he chose, could give the composers romantic librettos, agreeing exactly with the specifications you have laid down?

(L) Quite possibly, for he is a genuinely romantic poet, and as a matter of fact I recall having had a libretto of his in hand which was laid out in a genuinely romantic way, though overcrowded with material and too lengthy. If I am not mistaken, it was called the *Ungeheuer und der bezauberte Wald*.[8]

· (F) You remind me yourself of one difficulty with which you obstruct your librettists.

I have in mind the incredible brevity which you prescribe. All our effort to grasp and present properly, in really significant language, this or that situation, the outburst of this or that passion, is in vain; for the whole

---

[4] *Der Augenarzt*, comic opera by Adalbert Gyrowetz (1811); this too was reviewed by Hoffmann (*Allgemeine musikalische Zeitung*, December 1812).

[5] Perhaps the most familiar are *Doktor und Apotheker* (1786) and *Das rote Käppchen* (1790).

[6] *Das Neusonntagskind* (1793) and *Die Schwestern von Prag* (1794), comic operas by Wenzel Müller.

[7] *Der gestiefelte Kater* ("Puss in Boots"), satiric comedy in three acts, first published in Tieck's *Volksmärchen von Peter Lebrecht* (Berlin, 1797).

[8] "Musical Fairytale in Four Acts" (1798), written for J. F. Reichardt, who did not set it to music.

must be dispatched in a couple of lines which, into the bargain, must permit your turning and twisting them according to your good pleasure.

(L) May I say that the poet, like the scene painter, must cover his whole canvas, after designing it properly, in bold, powerful strokes, and that it is music which now places the whole in so correct a light and in such proper perspective that everything stands out as though alive and individual, apparently arbitrary brush strokes blending in figures that stride forth boldly.

(F) We ought then to supply only a sketch, not a poem?

(L) By no means. It is obvious, after all, that the librettist, with respect to the arrangement and management of the whole, must be guided by the rules of drama derived from the nature of the problem; at the same time he actually does need to make a special effort to arrange the scenes in such a way that the story unfolds clearly and plainly before the beholder's eyes. Almost without understanding a word, the beholder must be in a position to form an idea of the plot from what he sees happening. No dramatic poem needs this to such an extreme degree as does the opera, for, aside from the fact that, even when the words are sung most clearly, one still understands them less than when they are spoken, the music too entices the audience all too easily into other regions, and it is only by constant firing at the point in which the dramatic effect is to concentrate that one succeeds in hitting it. Now as regards the words, these will be most acceptable to the composer if they express the situation to be presented tersely and forcefully; no special elegance is required and above all no images.

(F) How about the everlasting similes of Metastasio?

(L) True, that man actually had the peculiar idea that a composer, especially in an aria, has always first to be stimulated by some poetic image or other. Hence his eternally repeated opening lines: "Come una tortorella, etc.," "Come spuma in tempesta, etc.," and often there actually occurred, at least in the accompaniment, the cooing of the dove, the foaming of the sea, etc.[9]

(F) Are we then, not only to avoid poetic elegance, but to be barred also from every detailed delineation of interesting situations? For example, the young hero goes off to war and takes leave of his stricken father, the old king, whose kingdom a conquering tyrant is shaking at its foundations; or a cruel fate separates an adoring youth from his beloved; are then the two to say nothing but "Farewell"?

---

[9] This variety of aria is ridiculed by Metastasio himself in the second intermezzo of his *Didone* *abbandonata*. Hoffmann's examples seem to be invented.

(L) Though the former may speak briefly of his courage, of his confidence in his just cause, though the latter may say to his beloved that life
without her is but slow death, the composer, who is inspired, not by words,
but by action and situation, will be satisfied if the inner state of the young
hero's or parting lover's soul is depicted in bold strokes. To keep to your
example, in what accents, penetrating deep into one's innermost self, have
the Italians, countless times already, sung the little word "Addio"! Of
what thousands and thousands of nuances musical expression is capable!
Is not this precisely the secret of music's miraculous power, that, just
where plain speech runs dry, it opens up an inexhaustible spring of means
of expression?

(F) According to this, so far as the words are concerned, the librettist
ought to aim at the most extreme simplicity, and it should suffice merely
to suggest the situations in a bold and noble way.

(L) Exactly; for, as I said, subject matter, action, situation must inspire the composer, not showy language, and, aside from the so-called
poetic images, each and every reflection is for him a real mortification.

(F) But surely you believe that I feel quite keenly how difficult it
will be to write a good libretto to your specifications? In particular, that
simplicity of expression . . .

(L) For you who are so given to word painting, it will no doubt be
difficult enough. But just as Metastasio, in my opinion, has shown in his
librettos precisely how an opera ought *not* to be written, so there are many
Italian poems which might be cited as perfect models of what song texts
ought to be. What could be simpler than stanzas like this one, known all
over the world:

> Almen se non poss'io
> Seguir l'amato bene,
> Affetti del cor mio,
> Seguitelo per me! [10]

What a suggestion of a nature torn by love and grief lies in these few
simple words, a suggestion which the composer can lay hold of, presenting
then the suggested inner state of the affections with the full force of musical expression. Indeed the particular situation in which these words are
to be sung will so stimulate his imagination that he will give his melody
a character all its own. For this same reason you will also find that the
most poetic composers have often set poetry that is even downright bad
quite magnificently to music. But in this case it was the genuinely operatic,

---

10 Metastasio, *La Clemenza di Tito*, II, v.

romantic subject matter that inspired them. As an example I give you Mozart's *Zauberflöte*.

Ferdinand was on the point of replying when in the street, right outside their windows, there was a call to arms. He seemed surprised; Ludwig, with a deep sigh, pressed his friend's hand to his breast, exclaiming:

Alas, Ferdinand, faithful, dearly beloved friend! What is to become of art in these rude, stormy times? Will it not perish, like a delicate plant vainly turning its head toward the dark cloud behind which the sun has vanished?

Alas, Ferdinand, for the golden days of our youth! Where have they gone? Everything worth while is being swept under in the swift stream that floods by, devastating the fields; from out its inky waves peer bloody corpses, and in the horror that converges on us we are carried along—we have no supports—our cry of terror echoes in empty space—a sacrifice to unbridled fury, we sink, past help, to the bottom!

Ludwig was silent, lost in thought. Ferdinand got up; took saber and helmet; stood before Ludwig, who gazed at him in bewilderment, like the god of war, armed for battle. Then an inspired expression passed over Ferdinand's features; his eyes shone with burning fire, and, raising his voice, he said:

Ludwig, what has become of you? Has then the dungeon air you have breathed here so long so wasted you that, ill and sickly, you would no longer feel the stimulating spring breeze that sweeps outside through clouds that shine in morning's golden glow?

Nature's children wallowed in brutish idleness, despising the finest gifts she offered them, treading them under foot in wanton obstinacy. Then angry Mother Nature wakened War, long asleep in her fragrant flower garden. Like a bronze giant he strode into the midst of the dissolute who, fleeing before his terrible voice, sought the protection of the mother in whom they had lost faith. But faith brought with it knowledge: Only in strength is health—from battle springs immortality, as life from death!

Yes, Ludwig, a fateful time has come; and, as though in the awe-inspiring depths of the old sagas which murmur to us strangely, like thunder in the distant gloaming, we plainly hear again the voice of Force, the eternally ruling passion—indeed, striding visibly into our lives, it stirs in us a faith to which the secret of our being is revealed.

The dawn is breaking, and inspired singers soar already in the fragrant breezes, announcing the godlike, praising it in song. The golden gates are open, and art and science kindle in a single ray the sacred impulse which brings mankind together in one faith. Hence, friend, turn your gaze heavenward—courage—confidence—faith!

Ferdinand embraced his friend. Ludwig picked up his full glass: "Eternally pledged to the higher existence in life and death!" "Eternally pledged to the higher existence in life and death!" Ferdinand repeated, and in a few moments his flying steed was already carrying him to the throngs which, lusting furiously for battle, cheering wildly, were advancing toward the enemy.

II

Composer-Critics of the Nineteenth Century

6. C. M. von Weber

In Carl Maria von Weber (1786–1826) we meet the prototype of the nine-teenth-century composer-critic. Burney and Reichardt were observers of the musical scene—Weber seeks to mold public opinion; with Burney and Reich-ardt, writing on music was an end in itself—with Weber it is merely a means. Nowhere is this more apparent than in the two little essays with which Weber introduced to the opera-going public of Prague (1815) and Dresden (1817) his "Dramatic and Musical Notices" of the new operas to be performed under his direction. The undertaking, he says, is novel and even somewhat daring. Yet the attempt has to be made, and it is his duty to make it: "The good old days when the blessings of general and lasting peace invited every man to dedi-cate his free time to the arts and sciences—those good old days were rudely ended long ago, and with them disappeared, of course, the sympathetic interest of the public, essential to the work of art."

The novel character of Weber's literary activity, and of the literary activity of those who followed him, will stand out no less clearly if we contrast it with that of such eighteenth-century musicians as Quantz, C. P. E. Bach, and Leo-pold Mozart, or with that of Fux and Rameau. On the one hand, technical essays addressed to the musical fraternity; on the other, *feuilletons* addressed to the general public. Such things as Weber's analyses of the chorale harmoniza-tions of J. S. Bach, as revised by Vogler, or his exchange with the poet Adolf Müllner, who had criticized Weber's setting of one of his poems, such things as the Berlioz treatise on instrumentation or Wagner's pamphlet on conducting —these are, for the nineteenth century, the exception and not the rule.

Himself the author of an unfinished novel, one fragment from which is in-corporated in the review translated below, Weber counted among his friends many of the leading writers of the day: E. T. A. Hoffmann, whom he had met in Bamberg as early as 1811 and with whom he maintained the most cordial relations for ten years; Wieland, whom he had learned to know in Weimar in 1812 and to whom he owed the subject of his *Oberon;* Tieck, to whose circle he belonged during his years in Dresden; Brentano and Arnim, the compilers of *Des Knaben Wunderhorn;* and Jean Paul, whose writings he had known from childhood and whom he was to meet at last during the summer of 1822, at the time of his work on *Euryanthe.* Gerald Abraham contributed a first-rate account of Weber's literary activity to the *Musical Quarterly* for January, 1934 ("Weber as Novelist and Critic," XX, 27–38).

On the Opera "Undine"[1]

[1817]

Adapted from the fairy tale of the same name by Friedrich, Baron de La Motte Fouqué, set to music by E. T. A. Hoffmann, and performed for the first time at the Royal Theatre in Berlin.[2]

No SOONER had I decided to say something publicly about this beautiful work than the possible forms of notices, reviews, or whatever one pleases to call them, passed involuntarily before my mind's eye, and I became aware of how uncommonly difficult it is to obtain from them a definite picture of the object appraised or anything like the impression that it is itself capable of making. For the most part, it seems to me, they either coincide with the ordinary judgments of society, where, without further demonstration, one party finds a thing good, another bad, while the more moderate neither condemn nor commend, the whole deriving weight and credibility only from the personality of the judge and from the confidence placed in him (again a partisan consideration); or they waste themselves, dissolved into tiny particles, entering, from a technical point of view, into details of the musical construction of such large works as do not come at once into everyone's hands. The greatest effects and beauties proceed solely from the manner of their disposition and combination; detached from their context, they nearly always lose their whole character, often, indeed, bearing witness seemingly against themselves in that, thus considered apart, they become well-nigh meaningless. Only very rarely can even the liveliest description make fully intelligible their true, organically connected coexistence with the remainder. It goes without saying that this opinion also is subject to various restrictions, and that especially where art works already matters of common knowledge are concerned, analysis of form and structure can only be salutary to those seeking improvement. In the present case, however, where the sole object is to call public attention to a work by attempting to suggest the intellectual sphere within which it moves and to represent in its distinctive outlines the shape that the composer has given it, it seems to me necessary that the critic begin by explaining how he himself sees, believes, and thinks, from which, then,

---

1 Text: *Allgemeine musikalische Zeitung,* XIX (1817), 201–208.
2 The first performance took place on August 3, 1816; by July 27, 1817, when the theater was destroyed by fire, the opera had been given four-teen times. An edition of the vocal score (edited by Hans Pfitzner) was published in 1908. In recent years there have been revivals in Aachen (1922), Bamberg (1926), and Leipzig (1933). [Loewenberg]

his readers can easily infer the extent to which they can subscribe to criticisms originating therein. With this in mind I think it wise to introduce my actual notice of the opera with the following fragment from one of my larger works,[a] the more so since it corresponds closely to the tendencies of the opera *Undine*.

For the proper appraisal of an art work moving in time there is needed that calm, dispassionate state of mind which, susceptible to every kind of impression, is to be carefully shielded from definite opinion or tendency of feeling, a certain receptivity for the material being treated alone excepted. Only thus is there given to the artist the simple power to draw our affections with *his* feelings and figures into the world which *he* has created and in which *he*, a powerful master of every passionate stimulus, causes us with *him* and through *him* to feel pain, pleasure, horror, joy, hope, and love. It will then be demonstrated clearly and almost at once whether he is capable of creating a great design which we will retain permanently in our hearts or whether, a creature of restlessly changing strokes of genius, he will let us be attracted by details while we forget the whole.

In no variety of art work is this so difficult to avoid—and consequently so often present—as in the opera. By opera I understand, of course, the opera which the German desires—an art work complete in itself, in which the partial contributions of the related and collaborating arts blend together, disappear, and, in disappearing, somehow form a new world.

As a rule a few striking numbers determine the success of the whole. Only rarely are these numbers, agreeably stimulating in the moment of their hearing, swallowed up at the end, as they properly should be, in the great general impression. For one must come first to admire the whole; then, on closer acquaintance, one may take pleasure in the beauty of the separate parts of which the whole is composed.

The nature and inner disposition of opera, a whole composed of wholes, gives rise to this great difficulty, which musical heroes alone succeed in overcoming. As a result of the form which is its right, each musical composition gives the impression of an independent, organic, self-contained unit. Yet, as a part of the whole, it must disappear when the whole is beheld; at the same time, displaying several surfaces simultaneously, it can and

---

a *Künstlerleben.* [Also called *Eine musikalische Reise* and *Tonkünstlers Leben.* Weber worked on this half-humorous, half-autobiographical novel intermittently from 1809 until 1820, but left it unfinished and published only fragments. It was to have run to 23 chapters; the present fragment is a part of Chapter 5. The most complete text is that in Georg Kaiser's edition of Weber's *Sämtliche Schriften* (Berlin & Leipzig, 1908), pp. 437-510.—Ed.]

should be many-sided (especially if it is an ensemble piece), a Janus head to be taken in at a glance.

In this lies the great, mysterious secret of music, a secret to be felt but not to be expressed; here are united the fluctuating and resisting natures of anger and of love, of ecstatic suffering; here sylph and salamander intermingle, embracing one another. In a word, what love is to man, music is to the arts and to mankind, for it is actually love itself, the purest, most ethereal language of the emotions, containing all their changing colors in every variety of shading and in thousands of aspects; *true only once,* but to be understood simultaneously by thousands of differently constituted listeners.

Though it appear in new and unusual forms, this truth of musical speech will in the end affirmatively assert its rights. The fate of every epoch-making and significant art work proves this sufficiently. What, for example, could have seemed more strange than Gluck's works at the time when everyone was overwhelmed and enervated by the sensual sea of Italian music? At this moment there are artistic errors that are on the point of overwhelming us again—in quite another way, to be sure, but perhaps in a not less dangerous way. As ruling principles the all-powerful conditions of our time have set up only the extremes—death and pleasure. Oppressed by the horrors of war, grown callous to misery of every sort, we have sought amusement only in aesthetic pleasures of the crudest kind.[3] The theater has become a puppet show at which, studiously avoiding the delightful, delighting emotional disturbance that accompanies the real enjoyment of an art work, we cause to be unwound before us a succession of scenes and are content to be tickled with trivial jests and melodies or to be taken in by inappropriate mechanical effects with neither point nor sense. Accustomed to the striking in everyday life, we are here too affected only by the striking. To follow the gradual development of a passion or an ingeniously motivated intensification of interest is called exhausting, tiresome, and—as the result of inattention—unintelligible.

As to the opera *Undine,* I had had to listen to judgments contradictory in every respect, prompted by the conditions just touched on. I sought as best I could to attain complete impartiality, although I could not at once prevent myself from looking forward to something significant, an expectation fully justified by Herr Hoffmann's literary writings. He who

3 The defeat of Napoleon in 1815 had brought real peace to the German states for the first time in Weber's memory. Until then he had lived always in the troubled environment reflected in his settings of poems from Theodor Körner's *Leyer und Schwert,* Opus 41, 42, and 43 (1814 to 1816) and in his cantata *Kampf und Sieg,* Opus 44 (1815), on the victory at Belle Alliance (Waterloo).

can penetrate Mozart's intention as he did, with his ardent flow of imagination and deep temperament, in the essay on *Don Giovanni* [4] (*Phantasiestücke in Callot's Manier*, Part I), can produce nothing downright mediocre; at the worst, he will beat against and even reshape the boundaries—he will not walk about within them idly.

The adaptation impressed the writer as a dramatized fairy tale in which many an inner connection might well have been more definitely and distinctly clarified. Herr von Fouqué knew the story only too well, and in such case there often occurs a sort of self-deception in which others, while recognizing it, believe. Still, it is by no means, as some allege, unintelligible.

The composer has brought the opera to life the more distinctly and clearly, with definite colors and outlines. It is actually *a single cast*, and after repeated hearings the writer recalls no passage which dispelled for him, even for a moment, the magic of the cycle of pictures which the composer had conjured up for him. Indeed, from beginning to end, he arouses so powerfully the interest in musical development that with the first hearing one has actually grasped the whole, while the detail disappears in genuinely artistic innocence and modesty.

With unusual self-denial, the greatness of which can be fully appreciated only by him who knows what it means to sacrifice the glory of momentary applause, Herr Hoffmann has disdained to enrich single numbers at the expense of the whole, so easy to do if one calls attention to them by broadening and enlarging their execution beyond that proper to them as members of the artistic body. He proceeds relentlessly, obviously led on by a desire to be always *true* and to intensify the life of the drama instead of retarding or arresting it in its rapid progress. Varied and strikingly portrayed as the many-sided characters of the persons of the action seem to be, they are all encircled by—or better, creatures of—that ghostly, fabulous world whose awesome stimulations are the peculiar property of the fairylike. Kühleborn stands out most prominently (the writer, like Fouqué, assumes a familiarity with the story) as a result of melodic selection and instrumentation which, remaining faithful to him throughout, announces his sinister presence. [5] Since he appears, if not as Destiny herself, then as the immediate agent of her will, this is after all quite correct. After him comes the lovely water sprite Undine, whose tonal waves now swirl and ripple, now, mightily threatening, assert their sovereign

---

[4] An excellent English translation, by Abram Loft, appeared in the *Musical Quarterly*, XXXI (1945), 504–516.

[5] As in *Don Giovanni*, and still to some extent in *Der Freischütz* and *The Flying Dutchman*, the use of the principle of the *leitmotiv* in Hoffmann's *Undine* is restricted to the supernatural.

power. A highly successful piece, her aria in Act II seems to the writer to sum up her whole character; uncommonly pleasing and ingeniously handled, it will serve as a small foretaste of the whole and is accordingly published here as a supplement.[b] The ardently fluctuating and unsteady Huldebrand, giving in to every lover's impulse, and the simple, pious Man of God, with his grave chorale melody, are then the most important. Berthalda, the Fisherman and Fishermaid, and the Duke and Duchess remain more in the background. The chorus of Attendants breathes joyous, pulsating life and in single numbers takes on an uncommonly satisfying freshness and gaiety, contrasting with the awesome choruses of the Spirits of Earth and Water, with their cramped and unusual progressions.

Most successful and quite grandly conceived seems to the writer the end of the opera, where the composer, as crown and capstone, has at length spread out the whole fullness of harmony in a pure eight-part double chorus and has pronounced the words "Now farewell to earthly care and pomp" with a real sense for their deeper meaning in a devoutly heartfelt melody that has a certain grandeur and melancholy sweetness, whereby the actually tragic ending leaves behind it a magnificent feeling of tranquillity. Enclosing the whole, overture and final chorus here join hands. The former builds up and discloses the wonder world, beginning quietly, then passionately storming along with growing intensity, immediately thereafter plunging directly into the action without coming to a full stop; the latter soothes and is perfectly satisfying. The whole work is one of the most ingenious that our day has given us. It is the magnificent result of the most perfect familiarity with, and grasp of, the subject, brought about by profoundly considered reflection and calculation of the effects of all the means of art, marked as a work of fine art by its beautiful and intimate melodic conception.

From all this it follows of itself that there are herein contained big instrumental effects, a knowledge of harmony, combinations often new, a correct declamation, with other necessary devices that are at the disposal of every real master, without a ready command of which there can be no freedom of thought.

And now, an observation as to what follows (for there must of course be blame as well as praise): The writer will not conceal certain wishes, although in *Undine* he would have *nothing* different, since everything, as it stands there, is necessary exactly as it is and not otherwise; one must needs wait to see whether the same things will reveal themselves in another work; one can, however, learn in a general way, by listening even

---

b It is to be supplied in a few weeks. [The promised supplement never appeared.—Ed.]

to *one* work, what those favorite devices are against which real friends ought to warn the composer, lest in the end they become mannerisms.

The writer, then, is struck by and wishes avoided: the partiality for little short figures which not only tend to become monotonous but easily oppress and obscure the melody, which, if it is to stand out, demands great experience and care on the part of the conductor; then, the partiality for the violoncellos and violas, for diminished-seventh chords, and for endings that are often too quickly broken off, which, at least on first hearing, are somewhat disturbing and, while by no means incorrect, for all that, inadequate; finally, certain inner voices which, because of their repeated employment by Cherubini, invite the vulgar to hunt for reminiscences.

As regards scenery and costume the performance may be pronounced splendid, and as regards singing and acting, a success. Regular capacity houses demonstrate the undiminishing, indeed constantly increasing interest that the opera has for the public. The prejudiced ascribe much to the scenery. But when the writer observes that in other pieces where this is the case people wait only for these moments and then leave, while here they remain, continuously and uniformly attentive, from beginning to end, the interest that the thing itself arouses in them is sufficiently proved. Tumultuous applause the composer could procure for nearly all the musical numbers by expanding a little the concluding measures; here the contrary obtains, and everything occurs swiftly and is constantly impelled forward.

May Herr Hoffmann soon give to the world again something as solid as this opera is, and may his many-sided talent, which within a short space of time brought him fame as an author and assured him the respect of his colleagues as a man of affairs (Councilor of the Royal Prussian Court of Appeals), become actively influential and productive in this branch of art also.

Written in Berlin, January, 1817.
Carl Maria von Weber.[6]

---

[6] At the time of the publication of this review, Hoffmann and Weber were still fast friends. Later on, after Hoffmann's work on the German libretto for Spontini's *Olimpie*, Weber's friendliness toward Hoffmann cooled, and the publication in the *Vossische Zeitung* of Hoffmann's masterly but distinctly critical review of *Der Freischütz* ended their association for good.

7. Hector Berlioz

In 1856, on Berlioz's election to the Institute, his friends were outraged and his enemies consoled by a malicious bon mot put into circulation by the music critic of the *Revue des deux mondes:* "Instead of a musician, the Institute has chosen a journalist." Yet a casual reader of the Parisian press of those days might almost have believed this true. Since 1823, Berlioz had been a regular contributor to one musical or literary review after another; by 1864, when he gave up his long-standing association with the *Journal des débats*, he had published more than 650 separate pieces—leading articles, letters from abroad, humorous sketches, fictitious anecdotes, imaginary conversations, *causeries* and *feuilletons* of every sort and description. Only a small part of this enormous production is assembled in his three volumes of collected writings—*Les soirées de l'orchestre* (1852), *Les grotesques de la musique* (1859), and *À travers chants* (1862); other pieces were salvaged in his *Voyage musical* (1844) and in the two volumes of his memoirs, printed in 1865 but not published until after his death.

"Music is not made for everyone, nor everyone for music"—this is perhaps the central article of Berlioz's critical creed, and in the essay translated below it recurs again and again with the persistence of an *idée fixe*. But in writing on *William Tell,* Berlioz also reveals many of the other facets of his critical personality—his preoccupation with the poetic and the picturesque, his capacity for enthusiasm and for indignation, his horror of the mediocre and his impatience with all that fails to measure up to the very highest standards, his contempt for everything academic, his intense dissatisfaction with the commercial and official aspects of musical life. Above all, he reveals his sense of justice and his readiness to acknowledge merit, even in the camp of the enemy. From the first, Berlioz had taken his stand with the opponents of Rossini and "the party of the dilettanti." But he has undertaken to review *William Tell* and he does so without *parti pris* and without hypocrisy.

Rossini's "William Tell" [1]

[*1834*]

TIRED OF hearing perpetual criticism of his works from the point of view of dramatic expression, still more tired, perhaps, of the blind admiration of his fanatical adherents, Rossini has found a very simple means of silencing the one and getting rid of the others. This has been to write a score—one seriously thought out, considered at leisure, and conscientiously executed from beginning to end in accordance with the requirements imposed upon all time by taste and good sense. He has written *William Tell*. This splendid work is thus to be regarded as an application of the author's new theories, as a sign of those greater and nobler capacities whose development the requirements of the sensual people for whom he has written until now have necessarily made impossible. It is from this point of view that we shall examine—without favor, but also without the least bias—Rossini's latest score.

If we consider only the testimonials that it has earned, the applause that it has called forth, and the conversions that it has made, *William Tell* has unquestionably had an immense success—a success that has taken the form of spontaneous admiration with some and of reflection and analysis with many others. And yet one is obliged to admit that to this glory it has not been able to add that other glory of which directors, and sometimes even authors, are more appreciative than of any other— popular success, that is, box-office success. The party of the dilettanti is hostile to *William Tell* and finds it cold and tiresome. The reasons for such a difference of opinion will become clear, we hope, in the course of the examination of this important production which we invite the reader to make with us. Let us follow the author step by step as he hurries along the new path that he has chosen, one that he would have reached the end of more rapidly and with a steadier pace if the force of deeply rooted habit had not caused him to cast an occasional glance behind him. These rare deviations once again bear out the old proverb: "In the arts one must take sides; there is no middle ground."

1 Text: *Gazette musicale de Paris*, I (1834), 326–327, 336–339, 341–343, 349–351. Berlioz's essay was not written until five years after the first performance of the opera, which took place in Paris on August 3, 1829.

For the first time Rossini has sought to compose an overture meeting the dramatic requirements recognized by every nation in Europe, Italy alone excepted. In making his debut in this style of instrumental music, entirely new to him, he has enlarged the form, so that his overture has in fact become a symphony in four distinct movements instead of the piece in two movements usually thought to be sufficient.

The first movement depicts most successfully, in our opinion, the calm of profound solitude, the solemn silence of nature when the elements and the human passions are at rest. It is a poetic beginning to which the animated scenes that are to follow form a most striking contrast—a contrast in expression, even a contrast in instrumentation, this first part being written for five solo violoncellos, accompanied by the rest of the basses and contrabasses, while the entire orchestra is brought into play in the next movement, "The Storm."

In this, it seems to us, our author would have done well to abandon the square-cut rhythms, the symmetrical phrase-structures, and the periodically returning cadences that he uses so effectively at all other times: "often a beautiful disorder is an effect of art," as an author says whose classical reserve is beyond question.[2] Beethoven proves this in the prodigious cataclysm of his Pastoral Symphony; at the same time he attains the end which the Italian composer lets us expect but does not give us. Several of the harmonic devices are remarkable and ingeniously brought in; among others, the chord of the minor ninth gives rise to effects that are indeed singular. But it is disappointing to rediscover in the storm scene of *William Tell* those staccato notes of the wind instruments which the amateurs call "drops of rain"; Rossini has already used this device in the little storm in the *Barber of Seville* and perhaps in other operas. In compensation he manages to draw from the bass drum without the cymbals picturesque noises in which the imagination readily rediscovers the re-echoing of distant thunder among the anfractuosities of the mountains. The inevitable decrescendo of the storm is handled with unusual skill. In short, it is not arresting or overpowering like Beethoven's storm, a musical tableau which will perhaps remain forever unequalled, and it lacks that sombre, desolate character which we admire so much in the introduction to *Iphigenia in Tauris*, but it is beautiful and full of majesty. Unfortunately the musician is always in evidence; we never lose sight of him in his combinations, even in those which seem the most eccentric. Beethoven on the other hand has known how to reveal himself wholly to the attentive listener: it is no longer an

---

2 Boileau, *L'Art poétique*, ii, 72.

orchestra that one hears, it is no longer music, but rather the tumultuous voice of the heavenly torrents blended with the uproar of the earthly ones, with the furious claps of thunder, with the crashing of uprooted trees, with the gusts of an exterminating wind, with the frightened cries of men and the lowing of the herds. This is terrifying, it makes one shudder, the illusion is complete. The emotion that Rossini arouses in the same situation falls far short of attaining the same degree of . . . But let us continue.

The storm is followed by a pastoral scene, refreshing in the extreme; the melody of the English horn in the style of the *ranz des vaches* is delicious, and the gamboling of the flute above this peaceful song is ravishing in its freshness and gaiety. We note in passing that the triangle, periodically sounding its tiny pianissimo strokes, is in its right place here; it represents the little bell sounded by the flocks as they saunter quietly along while the shepherds call and answer with their joyful songs. "So you find dramatic meaning in this use of the triangle," someone asks us; "in that case, pray be good enough to tell us what is represented by the violins, violas, basses, clarinets, and so forth." To this I should reply that these are musical instruments, essential to the existence of the art, while the triangle, being only a piece of iron whose sound does not belong to the class of sounds with definite pitch, ought not to be heard in the course of a sweet and tranquil movement unless its presence there is perfectly motivated, failing which it will seem only bizarre and ridiculous.

With the last note of the English horn, which sings the pastoral melody, the trumpets enter with a rapid incisive fanfare on b, the major third in the key of G, established in the previous movement, and in two measures this b becomes the dominant in E major, thus determining in a manner as simple as it is unexpected the tonality of the Allegro that follows. This last part of the overture is treated with a *brio* and a verve that invariably excite the transports of the house. Yet it is built upon a rhythm that has by now become hackneyed, and its theme is almost exactly the same as that of the Overture to *Fernand Cortez*. The staccato figuration of the first violins, bounding from C-sharp minor to G-sharp minor, is a particularly grateful episode, ingeniously interpolated into the midst of this warlike instrumentation; it also provides a means of returning to the principal theme and gives to this return an irresistible impetuosity which the author has known how to make the most of. The peroration of the saucy Allegro has genuine warmth. In short, despite its lack of originality in theme and rhythm, and despite its somewhat vulgar use of the bass drum, most disagreeable at certain moments, constantly pounding away on the strong beats as in a *pas redoublé* or the music of a country dance, one has to admit that the piece as a whole is treated with undeniable mastery and with an elan more captivating, perhaps, than any that Rossini has shown before, and that the Overture to *William Tell* is the work of an enormous talent, so much like genius that it might easily be mistaken for it.

Act I opens with a chorus that has a beautiful and noble simplicity. Placid joy is the feeling that the composer was to paint, and it is difficult to imagine anything better, more truthful, and at the same time more delicate than the melody he has given to these lines:

> How clear a day the skies foretell!
> Come bid it welcome with a song!

The vocal harmonies, supported by an accompaniment in the style of the *ranz des vaches*, breathe happiness and peace. Towards the end of the piece, the modulation from G to E-flat becomes original because of the way in which it is presented and makes an excellent effect.

The *romance* that follows ("Hasten aboard my boat") does not seem to us to be on the same level. Its melody is not always as naive as it should be for the song of a fisherman of Unterwald; many phrases are soiled by that affected style that the singers with their banal embellishments have unfortunately put into circulation. Besides, one scarcely knows why a Swiss should be accompanied by two harps.

Tell, who has been silent throughout the introduction and the fisherman's first stanza, comes forward with a measured monologue full of character; it sets before us the concentrated indignation of a lover of liberty, deeply proud of soul. Its instrumentation is perfect, likewise its modulations, although in the vocal part there are some intervals whose intonation is quite difficult.

At this point the general defect of the work as a whole begins to make itself felt. The scene is too long, and since the three pieces of which it consists are not very different in their coloring, the result is a tiring monotony which is further accentuated by the silence of the orchestra during the *romance*. In general, unless the stage is animated by a powerful dramatic interest, it is seldom that this kind of instrumental inactivity does not cause a fatal indifference, at least at the Opéra. Aside from this, the house is so enormous that a single voice, singing way at the back of the stage, reaches the listener deprived of that warm vibrancy that is the life of music and without which a melody can seldom stand out clearly and make its full effect.

After the intoning of a *ranz des vaches* with its echoes, in which four horns in G and E represent the Alpine trumpet, an Allegro vivace revives the attention. This is a chorus, full of impassioned verve, and it would be admirable if the meaning of the text were just the opposite of what it actually is. The key is E minor and the melody is so full of alarm and agitation that at the first performance, not hearing the words, as usually happens in large theatres, I expected the news of some catastrophe —at the very least, the assassination of Father Melchthal. Yet, far from it, the chorus sings:

> From the mountains a summons
> To repose sounds a call;
> A festival shall lighten
> Our labors in the field.

It is the first time that Rossini has been guilty of this particular kind of incongruity.

After this chorus, which is the second in this scene, there follows an accompanied recitative and then a third chorus, *maestoso*, chiefly remarkable for the rare felicity of the scale from the b in the middle register to the high b which the soprano spreads obliquely against the harmonic background. But the action does not progress, and this defect is made still more glaring by a fourth chorus, rather more violent than joyous in character, sung throughout in full voice, scored throughout for full orchestra, and accompanied by great strokes of the bass drum on the first beat of each measure. Wholly superfluous from the dramatic point of view, the piece has little musical interest. Ruthless cuts have been made in the present score, yet great care has been taken to delete nothing here; this would have been too reasonable. Those who make cuts know only how to cut out the good things; in castrating, it is precisely the noblest parts that are removed. By actual count, then, there are four fully developed choruses here, to do honor to "the clear day" and "the rustic festival," to celebrate "labor and love," and to speak of "the horns that re-echo close by the roaring torrents." This is an awkward blunder, especially at the beginning, this monotony in the choice of means, wholly unjustified by the requirements of the drama, whose progress it aimlessly brings to a standstill. It appears that the work has been dominated at many points by the same unfortunate influence which led the composer astray at this one. I say "the composer," for a man like Rossini al-

ways gets what he wants from his poet, and it is well known that for
William Tell he insisted on a thousand changes which M. Jouy did not
refuse him.

Lack of variety even affects the melodic style: the vocal part is full
of repeated dominants, and the composer turns about the fifth step of
the scale with tiresome persistence, as though it held for him an almost
irresistible attraction. Here are some examples from Act I. During the
fanfare of the four horns in E-flat, Arnold sings:

> Have a care! Have a care!
> The approach of the Austrian tyrant
> Is announced by the horns from the mountain.

All these words are on a single note—b-flat. In the duet that follows,
Arnold again resorts to this b-flat, the dominant in E-flat, for the recita-
tion of two whole lines:

> Under the yoke of such oppression
> What great heart would not be cast down?

Further on, after the modulation to D minor, Tell and Arnold sing alternately on a, the dominant of the new key:

> TELL: Let's be men and we shall win!
> ARNOLD: What revenge can end these affronts?
> TELL: Ev'ry evil rule is unstable.

Against this obstinate droning of the dominant, the five syllables on d,
f, and c-sharp at the ends of the phrases can barely be made out. The key
changes to F, and the dominant, c, appears again immediately:

> ARNOLD: Think of all you may lose!
> TELL: No matter!
> ARNOLD: What acclaim can we hope from defeat?

And later on:

> ARNOLD: Your expectation?
> TELL: To be victorious,
> And yours as well; I must know what you hope.

Nor is this all; the dominants continue:

> When the signal sounds for the combat,
> My friend, I shall be there.

The E-flat fanfare of the horns begins again and Tell exclaims:

> The signal! Gessler comes.
> Even now as he taunts us,
> Willing slave of his whim, are you waiting
> To entreat the disdain of a favoring glance?

These four lines are entirely on the dominant, b-flat. True to his favorite note, Tell again returns to it in order to say, near the end of the movement:

> The music calls; I hear the wedding chorus;
> Oh, trouble not the shepherds at their feast
> Nor spoil their pleasures with your sad lament!

A defect as serious as this does immense harm to the general effect of the fine duet. I say "fine," for despite this chiming of dominants, it is really admirable in all other respects: the instrumentation is treated with unusual care and delicacy; the modulations are varied; Arnold's melody ("Oh Mathilda, my soul's precious idol") is suave in the extreme; many of Tell's phrases are full of dramatic accents; and except for the music of the line "But at virtue's call I obey," the whole has great nobility.

The pieces that follow are all of them more or less noteworthy. We cite in preference the A minor chorus:

> Goddess Hymen,
> Thy bright feast day
> Dawns for us.

This would have a novel, piquant effect if it were sung as one has the right to demand that all choruses should be at the Royal Academy of Music. The pantomimic Allegro of the archers also has great energy, and several *airs de danse* are distinguished by their fresh melodies and the exceptional finish of their orchestration.

The grand finale which crowns the act seems to us much less satisfactory. The beginning brings in the voices and orchestra a return of the dominant pedal-points which have been absent for some time. After a few exclamations by the chorus of Swiss, one hears Gessler's soldiers:

> The hour of justice now is striking.
> The murd'rer be accursed!
> No quarter!

All this is recited on b, the dominant in E minor, which has already been used as a pedal by the basses of the orchestra during the first nineteen measures of the introduction. Confronted by this persistent tendency of the composer's to fall back on the most familiar and monotonous of musical formulas, one can only suppose it to be due to sheer laziness. It is very practical indeed to write a phrase for orchestra whose harmony turns about the two fundamental chords of the key and then, when one has a left-over bit of text to add to it, to set this to the dominant, the note common to the two chords—this saves the composer much time and trouble. After this introductory movement there follows a chorus ("Virgin, adored by ev'ry Christian"); the tempo is slow—I might say, almost dragging—and the piece is accompanied in a very ordinary fashion, so that its effect is to hold up the action and the musical interest most inappropriately. Little is added by the syllabic asides of the soldiers' chorus during the singing of the women:

> How they tremble with fright!
> Do as we bid!
> Your own lives are at stake!

The music for these words is neither menacing nor ironic—it is simply a succession of notes, mere padding to fill out the harmonies, expressing neither contempt nor anger. At length, when the women have finished their long prayer, Rudolf—Gessler's most ardent satellite—breaks out in a violent rage. The orchestra takes a tumultuous headlong plunge, the trombones bellow, the violins utter shrill cries, the instruments vie with one another in elaborating "the horrors of plundering and pillage" with which the Swiss are threatened; unfortunately, the whole is a copy of the finale of *La Vestale*. The figuration of the basses and violas, the strident chords of the brass, the incisive scales of the first violins, the syllabic accompaniment of the second chorus beneath the broad melody of the soprano—Spontini has them all. Let us add, however, that the *stretta* of this chorus contains a magnificent effect due wholly to Rossini. It is the syncopated descending scale for the whole chorus, singing in octaves, while trebles, flutes, and first violins forcefully sustain the major third e to g-sharp; against this interval the notes d-sharp, a, and f-sharp of the lower voices collide in violent agitation. This idea alone, in its grandeur and force, completely effaces all previous sections of the finale. These are now wholly forgotten. At the beginning one was indifferent—in the end one is moved; the author seemed to lack invention—he has redeemed himself and astonished us with an unexpected stroke. Rossini is full of such contrasts.

The curtain rises on Act II. We are witnesses of a hunt; horses cross the stage at a gallop. The fanfare which we heard two or three times during the preceding act resounds again; it is differently scored, to be sure, and linked to a characteristic chorus, but it is a misfortune that so undistinguished a theme should be heard so frequently. The development of the drama imposed it, the musician will tell us. Nevertheless, as we have said before, Rossini might have obtained from his librettist a different arrangement of the scenes and thus have avoided these numerous chances of monotony. He failed to do so and, now that it is too late, he regrets it. Let us go on. Halfway through the chorus just mentioned there is a diatonic passage played in unison by the horns and the four bassoons that has an energy all its own, and the piece as a whole would be captivating were it not for the torture inflicted upon the listener who is at all sensitive by the innumerable strokes of the bass drum on the strong beats, whose effect is the more unfortunate since they again call attention to rhythmic constructions that are completely lacking in originality.

To all this I am sure that Rossini will reply: "Those constructions which seem to you so contemptible are precisely the ones that the public understands the most readily." "Granted," I should answer; "but if you profess so great a respect for the propensities of the vulgar, you ought also to limit yourself to the most commonplace things in melody, harmony, and instrumentation. This is just what you have taken care not to do. Why, then, do you condemn rhythm alone to vulgarity? Besides, in the arts, criticism cannot and should not take account of considerations of this kind. Am I on the same footing as an amateur who hears an opera once every three or four months, I who have occupied myself exclusively with music for so many years? Haven't my ears become more delicate than those of the student whose hobby it is to play flute duets on Sundays? Am I as ignorant as the shopkeeper on the Rue Saint-Denis? In a word, do you not admit that there is progress in music, and in criticism a quality that distinguishes it from blind instinct, namely taste and judgment? Of course you do. This being the case, the ease or difficulty with which the public understands new departures counts for little; this has to do with material results, with business, while it is art that concerns us. Besides, the public—especially in Paris—is not as stupid as some would like to think; it does not reject innovations if they are presented with the right sort of candor. The people who are hostile to innovations are—need I name them?—the *demi-savans*. No, frankly; excuses of this kind are inacceptable. You have written a commonplace rhythm, not because the public would have rejected another, but because it was easier and above all quicker to repeat what had already been used over and over again than to search for more novel and more distinguished combinations."

The distant "Bell Chorus," a contrast in style to the chorus that preceded it, seems to bear out this opinion of ours. Here the whole is full of charm—pure, fresh, and novel. The end of the piece even presents a chord-succession whose effect is delightful, although the harmonies succeed one another in an order prohibited by every rule adopted since the schools began. I refer to the diatonic succession of triads in parallel motion which occurs in connection with the fourfold repetition of the line, "The night has come." A Master of Musical Science would call this kind of part-writing most incorrect: the basses and first sopranos are continually at the octave, the basses and second sopranos continually at the fifth. After the C major triad come those in B major and A minor and finally that in G major, the prevailing tonic. The agreeable effect resulting from these four consecutive fifths and octaves is due, in the first place, to the short pause that separates the chords, a pause sufficient to isolate the harmonies one from another and to give to each fundamental the aspect of a new tonic; in the second place, to the naive coloring of the piece, which not only authorizes this infraction of a time-honored rule, but makes it highly picturesque. Beethoven has already written a similar succession of triads in the first movement of his Eroica; everyone knows the majestic nobility of this passage. Believe then, if you must, in absolute rules!

Hardly has this evening hymn died away like a graceful sunset when we are greeted with another return of the horn fanfare with its inevitable pedal-point on the dominant:

> There sounds a call, the horn of Gessler.
> It bids us return; we obey it.

The chief huntsman and the chorus recite these two lines in their entirety on b-flat. Our earlier observations have here a more direct and a more particular application.

With the following number the composer begins a higher flight; this is quite another style. Mathilda's entrance is preceded by a long ritornello doubly interesting as harmony and as dramatic expression. There is real passion in this, and that feverish agitation that animates the heart of a young woman obliged to conceal her love. Then comes a recitative, perfect in its diction and admirably commented upon by the orchestra, which reproduces fragments of the ritornello. After this introduction follows the well-known *romance*, "Sombre forests."

Rossini has, in our opinion, written few pieces as elegant, as fresh, as distinguished in their melody, and as ingenious in their modulations as this one: aside from the immense merit of the vocal part and the harmony, it involves a style of accompaniment for the violas and first violins that is full of melancholy, also—at the beginning of each stanza—a pianissimo effect for the kettledrum that rouses the listener's attention in a lively manner. One seems to hear one of those natural sounds whose cause remains unknown, one of those strange noises which attract our attention on a clear day in the deep forest and which redouble in us the feeling of silence and isolation. This is poetry, this is music, this is art—beautiful, noble, and pure, just as its votaries would have it always.

This style is sustained until the end of the act, and from henceforth marvel follows marvel. In the duet between Arnold and Mathilda, so full of chevaleresque passion, we mention as a blemish the long pedal of the horns and trumpets on g, alternately tonic and dominant, the effect of which is at certain moments atrocious. Then too we shall reproach the composer for having blindly followed the example of the older French composers, who would have thought themselves disgraced if they had failed to bring in the trumpets at once whenever the words made any mention of glory or victory. In this respect Rossini treats us like the dilettanti of 1803,[8] like the admirers of Sédaine and Monsigny.

> Ah, return to war and to glory,
> Take wing and make me proud once more!
> One gains a name if one's a victor;
> The world will then approve my choice.

"Out with the obbligato fanfare," Rossini will have said on reading this in his libretto; "I am writing for France." Finally, it seems to us that this duet, which is developed at considerable length, would gain if there were no repetition of the motive which the two singers have together, "The one who adores you." Since the tempo of this passage is slower than the rest, the repetition necessarily brings with it two interruptions which break up the general pace and detract from the animated effect of the scene by prolonging it uselessly.

But from this point until the final chord of the second act, this defect does not recur. Walter and Tell enter unexpectedly; Mathilda takes flight, Arnold remains to listen to bitter reproaches on his love for the daughter of the Helvetian tyrant. Nothing could be more beautiful, more expressive, more noble than this recitative, both in the vocal parts and in the orchestra. Two phrases are particularly striking in the verity of their expression. One is Walter's counsel:

---

8 The year in which Berlioz was born.

> Perhaps, though, you should alter
> And take the pains to know us better.

The other is Tell's apostrophe:

> Do you know what it is to feel love for one's country?

At length, the tragic ritornello of the trio is unfolded. Here we confess that, despite our role as critic and the obligations that it brings with it, it is impossible for us to apply the cold blade of the scalpel to the heart of this sublime creation. What should we analyze? The passion, the despair, the tears, the lamentations of a son horrified by the news of his father's murder? God forbid! Or should we make frivolous observations about details, quibble with the author over a *gruppetto* or a solo passage for the flute or an obscure moment in the second violin part? Not I! If others have the courage for it, let them attempt it. As for me, I have none at all—I can only join the crowd in shouting: "Beautiful! Superb! Admirable! Ravishing!"

But I shall have to be sparing of my enthusiastic adjectives, for I am going to need them for the rest of the act, which remains almost continuously on this same high level. The arrival of the three cantons affords the composer an opportunity to write three pieces in three wholly different styles. The first chorus is in a strong, robust style which paints for us a working people with calloused hands and arms that never tire. In the second chorus and the chaste sweetness of its melody we recognize the timid shepherds; the expression of their fears is ravishing in its grace and naïveté. The fishermen from the canton of Uri arrive by boat from the lake while the orchestra imitates as faithfully as music can the movements and the cadenced efforts of a crew of oarsmen. Hardly have these late-comers disembarked when the three choruses unite in a syllabic ensemble, rapidly recited in half voice and accompanied by the pizzicati of the strings and an occasional muffled chord from the wind instruments:

> Before you, Tell, you see
> Three peoples as one band,
> Our rights our only arms
> Against a vile oppressor.

First recited by the chorus of fishermen and then taken up by the two other choruses, who mingle with it their exclamations and their laconic asides, this phrase is dramatically most realistic. Here is a crowd in which each individual, moved by hope and fear, can scarcely hold back the sentiments that agitate him, a crowd in which all wish to speak and each man interrupts his neighbor. Be it said in passing that the execution of this *coro parlato* is extremely difficult, a fact that may in part excuse the choristers of the Opéra, who usually recite it very badly indeed.

But Tell is about to speak and all grow silent—*arrectis auribus adstant.*[4] He stirs them, he inflames them, he apprises them of Melchthal's cruel death, he promises them arms; finally he asks them directly:

> TELL: Do you agree to help?
> CHORUS: We one and all agree.
> TELL: You will join us?
> CHORUS: We will.
> TELL: Even in death?
> CHORUS: We will.

Then, uniting their voices, they swear a grave and solemn oath to "the God of kings and of shepherds" to free themselves from slavery and to exterminate their tyrants. Their gravity under these circumstances, which would be absurd if they were Frenchmen or Italians, is admirable for a cold-blooded people like the Swiss, whose decisions, if less precipitate, are not lacking in steadfastness or in assurance of attainment. The movement becomes animated only at the end, when Arnold catches sight of the first rays of the rising sun:

> ARNOLD: The time has come.
> WALTER: For us this is a time of danger.
> TELL: Nay, of vict'ry!
> WALTER: What answer shall we give him?
> ARNOLD: To arms!
> ARNOLD ⎫
> TELL   ⎬ To arms!
> WALTER ⎭

Then the whole chorus, the soloists, the orchestra, and the percussion instruments, which have not been heard since the beginning of the act, one and all take up the cry: "To arms!" And at this last and most terrible war cry which bursts forth from all these breasts, shivering in the dawn of the first day of liberty, the entire instrumental mass hurls itself like an avalanche into an impetuous Allegro!

Ah, it is sublime! Let us take breath.

We left Arnold in despair, thinking only of war and vengeance. His father's death, imposing new obligations upon him, has torn him abruptly from the attraction that had lured him little by little towards the ranks

---

4 They stand by with attentive ears.—Vergil. *Aeneid.* i. 152. [Fairclough]

of his country's enemies. Filled with gloomy thoughts, his words to Mathilda at the beginning of Act III reveal his fierce and sombre pre-occupation:

> ARNOLD: I tarry to avenge my father.
> MATHILDA: What is your hope?
> ARNOLD: It is blood that I hope for;
> I renounce Fortune's favors all,
> I renounce all love and all friendship,
> Even glory, even marriage.
> MATHILDA: And I, Melchthal?
> ARNOLD: My father's dead.

The expression of these agitated sentiments dominates the whole of the long ritornello which precedes and prepares the entrance of the two lovers. After a short but energetic recitative, in which Arnold sings an-other five-measure phrase on a single note, an e, the great agitato aria of Mathilda begins.

At the outset, this piece is not as happy in its choice of melody and in its dramatic expression as we find it at the end. The composer seems to have begun it in cold blood and to have come to life by degrees as he pene-trated his subject. The first phrase is what we might call "a phrase in compartments" (une phrase à compartimens); it belongs to that vast family of melodies consisting of eight measures, four of them on the tonic and as many on the dominant, examples of which occur at the be-ginning of nearly every concerto of Viotti, Rode, Kreutzer, and their imitators. This is a style in which each development can be foreseen well in advance; in composing this, his latest and perhaps his most important work, it would seem to us that Rossini ought to have abandoned it once and for all. Aside from this, the two lines that follow cry out for an expressive musical setting:

> In my heart solitude unending!
> Shall you never be at my side?

Rossini has failed to give it to them. What he has written is cold and commonplace, despite an instrumentation that might have been less tor-tured in its superabundant luxuriousness. As though to efface the memory of this somewhat scholastic beginning, the peroration is admirable in its originality, its grace, and its sentiment. The liveliest imagination could not have asked the composer for a style of declamation more truthful or more noble than that in which he has caused Mathilda to exclaim, with melancholy abandon:

To the land of the stranger
Whose shore you seek, I may not follow
To offer you my tender care,
And yet all my heart shall be with you,
To all your woes it shall be true.

We are not as satisfied with the ensemble for the two voices which closes the scene. As the farewell of two lovers who separate, never to see one another again, it should have been heart-breaking; apart from Mathilda's chromatic vocalization on the word "Melchthal," it is only brilliant and overscored for the wind instruments, without contrasts or oppositions.

At the same time, it is greatly to be regretted—even if only because of the fine flashes of inspiration which we have mentioned—that the scene is entirely suppressed in the performances being given today. At present the act begins with the chorus of Gessler's soldiers, who are engaged in a brutal and arrogant celebration of the hundredth anniversary of the conquest of Switzerland and its addition to the German Empire.

After this there is dancing, of course; at the Opéra, an excuse for a ballet would be found, even in a representation of the Last Judgment. What difference does it make?—the *airs de danse,* all of them saturated with the Swiss melodic idiom, have rare elegance and are written with care (I except only the Allegro in G called the "Pas de soldats"). It is in the midst of this ballet that we meet the celebrated Tyrolienne, so popular nowadays, remarkable for its modulations and for the vocal rhythm which serves as its accompaniment. Before Rossini, no one writing for the stage had thought of using an immediate succession of chords having the character of contrasted tonic harmonies, such as the one that occurs in the thirty-third measure, where the melody outlines an arpeggio within the major triad on b, only to fall back at once into the one on g, the true tonic. This little piece, doubtless written one morning at the breakfast table, has had a truly incredible success, while beauties of an incomparably higher order have won only very limited approval, although this approval is, to be sure, of quite another sort than that which has welcomed the pretty Tyrolienne so graciously. With some composers, the applause of the crowd is useful but scarcely flattering—for these artists, only the opinion of the discriminating has real value. With others it is just the opposite—only quantity has value, while quality is almost worthless. Until their more frequent dealings with Europeans taught them the value of money, the American Indians preferred a hundred sous to a single gold piece.

After the dances comes the famous scene of the apple. Its style is in general nervous and dramatic. One of Tell's phrases in his dialogue with Gessler seems to us to have real character:

> GESSLER: My captive shall he be.
> TELL: Let us hope he may be your last.

On the other hand, a movement that seems to us absolutely false in sentiment and expression is that in which Tell, concerned for his son, takes him aside, embraces him, and orders him to leave:

> My heart's dearest treasure,
> Receive my embraces,
> Then depart from me.

Instead of this, it would have been enough to have made him a sign and to have uttered quickly these two words: "Save thyself!" To elaborate upon this idea in an Andante would perhaps have done no harm in an Italian opera, a really Italian one, but in a work like *William Tell*, where reason has been admitted to full civic rights, where not everything is directed towards permitting the singers to shine, such a piece is more than an incongruity—it is an outright nonsense.

The recitative that follows exactly meets the requirements that we have just laid down:

> Rejoin your mother! These my orders:
> That the flame on the mountains now be lighted
> To give to our allies the command to rebel.

This precipitate utterance throws an even more glaring light on the faulty expression that shocked us when this idea was presented before. In compensation, the composer offers us Tell's touching instructions to his little son:

> Move not a muscle, be calm and fearless,
> In prayer bend a suppliant knee!

How admirably the accompaniment of the violoncellos weeps beneath the voice of this father whose heart is breaking as he embraces his boy! The orchestra, almost silent, is heard only in pizzicato chords, each group followed by a rest of half a measure. The bassoons, pianissimo, sustain long plaintive notes. How filled all this is with emotion and anguish—how expressive of the anticipated great event about to be accomplished!

> My son, my son, think of thy mother!
> Patiently she waits for us both.

These last phrases of the melody are irresistibly lifelike; they go straight to the heart.

Let the partisans of popular opinion say what they please. If this sublime inspiration arouses only polite and infrequent applause, there is something about it that is nobler, higher, worthier for a man to take pride in having created, than there is in a graceful Tyrolienne, even though it be applauded by a hundred thousand and sung by the women and children of all Europe. There is a difference between the pretty and the beautiful. To pretend to side with the majority, and to value prettiness at the expense of that which addresses itself to the heart's most intimate sentiments, this is the part of the shrewd businessman, but not that of the artist conscious of his dignity and independence.

The finale of this act includes, in its first section, an admirably energetic passage which is invariably annihilated at the Opera by the inadequacy of the singer; this is the sudden outburst of the timid Mathilda:

> I claim him as my ward in the name of the sov'reign.
> In indignation a people is watching,
> Take care, take care, he is safe in my arms.

This general indignation is skillfully portrayed, both in the vocal part and in the orchestra; it is as lifelike as Gluck and Spontini. As an accompaniment to the ingeniously modulated melody of the sopranos, the syllabic theme of the men's chorus ("When their pride has misled them") makes an excellent effect. On the other hand, the *stretta* of this chorus consists only of furious cries; to be sure, they are motivated by the text, but they arouse no emotion in the listener, whose ears are needlessly outraged. Here again, it would perhaps have been better to change the wording of the libretto, for it would be difficult if not impossible to set the line, "Curséd be Gessler's name," except as a savage vociferation having neither melody nor rhythm and paralyzing by its violence all feeling for harmony.

Act IV re-establishes the individual passions and affords a needed relaxation after the uproar of the preceding scenes. Arnold revisits his father's deserted cottage; his heart filled with a hopeless love and with projects of vengeance, all his senses stirred by the recollections of bloody carnage always before his mind's eye, he breaks down, overcome by the enormity of the affecting contrast. All is calm and silent. Here is peace —and the tomb. And yet an infinity separates him from that breast upon which, at a moment like this, he would so gladly pour out his tears of filial piety, from that heart close to which his own would beat less sadly. Mathilda shall never be his. The situation is poetic, even poignantly melancholy, and it has inspired the musician to write an air which we do not hesitate to pronounce the most beautiful of the entire score. Here the young Melchthal pours out all the sufferings of his soul; here his mournful recollections of the past are painted in the most ravishing of melodies; harmony and modulation are employed only to reinforce the melodic expression, never out of purely musical caprice.

The Allegro with choruses, which follows, is full of spirit and makes a worthy crown for an equally fine scene. At the same time, the piece has only a very indifferent effect upon the public, to judge from the applause with which it is received. For the many it is too refined; delicate shadings like these nearly always escape their attention. Alas, if one could only reduce the public to an assembly of fifty sensible and intelligent persons, how blissful it would be to be an artist!

Since the first performance, the trio accompanied only by the wind instruments has been suppressed, also the piece immediately following it, the prayer sung during the storm. The cut is most inopportune, particularly in view of the prayer, a masterpiece in the picturesque style, whose musical conception is novel enough to have warranted some allowance being made in its favor. Aside from the *mise en scène*, considerations having to do with the decor or the stage machinery were no doubt responsible for the suppression of this interesting part of the score. The thing was accordingly done without hesitation—everyone knows that at the Opéra the directors *support* the music.

From this moment until the final chorus, we shall find nothing but padding. The outbursts of the orchestra while Tell struggles on the lake with the storm, the fragments of recitative interrupted by the chorus— these are things that the musician writes with confidence that no one will listen to them.

The final chorus is another story:

> About us all changes and grows.
> Fresh the air!

This is a beautiful harmonic broadening-out. The *ranz des vaches* floats gracefully above these massive chords and the hymn of Free Switzerland soars upward to heaven, calm and imposing, like the prayer of a just man.

8. Robert Schumann

In contrast to Weber, the practical propagandist, and Berlioz, the professional man of letters, Schumann brings to his critical writing romantic idealism and a high purpose. As he tells us himself in his introductory essay, the founding of the *Neue Zeitschrift* in 1834 was a direct outgrowth of his dissatisfaction with the existing state of music and of his desire to bring about a rehabilitation of the poetic principle, "the very thing," as he said later on, "by which we should like to have these pages distinguished from others." The editorial position of the new journal is perhaps most forcefully summed up in Schumann's "speech from the throne" for 1839: "A stern attitude towards foreign trash, benevolence towards aspiring younger artists, enthusiasm for everything masterly that the past has bequeathed." On the whole, these aims are not so very different from those implicit in Berlioz; it is simply that Schumann has less self-interest and less worldly wisdom and that he goes about his task in a more serious way, more humbly and more charitably, if also with greater chauvinism.

"The present is characterized by its parties," Schumann writes in another connection (1836). "Like the political present, one can divide the musical into liberals, middlemen, and reactionaries, or into romanticists, moderns, and classicists. On the right sit the elderly—the contrapuntists, the anti-chromaticists; on the left the youthful—the revolutionaries in their Phrygian caps, the anti-formalists, the genially impudent, among whom the Beethovenians stand out as a special class; in the *Juste Milieu* young and old mingle irresolutely—here are included most of the creations of the day, the offspring which the moment brings forth and then destroys."

In his day, Schumann stood at the very center of the romantic movement in German music, yet he makes little effort to define its aims and aspirations for us. To him, clearly, these were self-evident: "It is scarcely credible that a distinct romantic school could be formed in music, which is in itself romantic." But in his review of Stephen Heller's Opus 7 (1837) Schumann comes as close as he ever does to a definition and in so doing defines for us also his own personal style. "I am heartily sick of the word 'romanticist,' " he says; "I have not pronounced it ten times in my whole life; and yet—if I wished to confer a brief designation upon our young seer, I should call him one, and what a one! Of that vague, nihilistic disorder behind which some search for romanticism, and of that crass, scribbling materialism which the French neo-romanticists affect, our composer—thank Heaven!—knows nothing; on the contrary, he perceives things naturally, for the most part, and expresses himself clearly and judiciously. Yet on taking up his compositions one senses that there is something more than this lurking in the background—an attractive, individual half-light, more like dawn than dusk, which causes one to see his otherwise clear-cut configurations under an unaccustomed glow. . . . And do not let me overlook the dedication—the coincidence is astonishing. You recall, Eusebius, that we once dedicated something to the Wina of the *Flegeljahre*; the dedication of these impromptus also names one of Jean Paul's constellations —Liane von Froulay [in Jean Paul's *Titan*]. We have in general much in common, an admission that no one should misinterpret—it is too obvious."

Davidsbündlerblätter [1]

INTRODUCTORY

[*1854*]

NEAR THE end of the year 1833 there met in Leipzig, every evening and as though by chance, a number of musicians, chiefly younger men, primarily for social companionship, not less, however, for an exchange of ideas about the art which was for them the meat and drink of life—Music. It cannot be said that musical conditions in Germany were particularly encouraging at the time. On the stage Rossini still ruled, at the piano, with few rivals, Herz and Hünten. And yet only a few years had elapsed since Beethoven, Weber, and Schubert had lived among us. Mendelssohn's star was in the ascendant, to be sure, and marvelous reports were heard of a Pole, one Chopin—but it was not until later that these exerted lasting influence. Then one day an idea flashed across the minds of these young hotheads: Let us not sit idly by; let us attack, that things may become better; let us attack, that the poetic in art may again be held in honor! In this way the first pages of a "New Journal for Music" came into being. But the joy of the solid unanimity of this union of young talents did not continue long. In one of the most cherished comrades, Ludwig Schunke,[2]

---

1 Text: *Gesammelte Schriften über Musik und Musiker* (Leipzig, 1854); for the essay "New Paths," *Neue Zeitschrift für Musik*, XXXIX (1853), 185–186.

2 Talented composer and pianist, friend of Schumann's, co-editor of the *Zeitschrift* during its first year, Schunke died on December 7, 1834, shortly before his twenty-fourth birthday.

death claimed a sacrifice. As to the others,[3] some removed from Leipzig altogether for a time. The undertaking was on the point of dissolution. Then one of their number, precisely the musical visionary of the company, one who had until now dreamed away his life more at the piano than among books, decided to take the editing of the publication in hand; [4] he continued to guide it for nearly ten years, to the year 1844. So there arose a series of essays, from which this volume offers a selection. The greater part of the views therein expressed are still his today. What he set down, in hope and fear, about many an artistic phenomenon has in the course of time been substantiated.

Here ought also to be mentioned another league, a more than secret one in that it existed only in the head of its founder—the "Davidsbünd-ler." In order to represent various points of view within the view of art as a whole, it seemed not inappropriate to invent contrasted types of artist, among which Florestan and Eusebius were the most significant, be-tween whom Master Raro stood as intermediary. Like a red thread, this "Davidsbündler" company wound itself through the journal, humorously blending "Wahrheit und Dichtung." [5] Later on, these comrades, not un-welcome to the readers of that time, disappeared entirely from the paper, and from the time when a Peri enticed them into distant climes, nothing further has been heard of their literary efforts.

Should these collected pages, while reflecting a highly agitated time, likewise contribute to divert the attention of those now living to artistic phenomena already nearly submerged by the stream of the present, the aim of their publication will have been fulfilled.

· · · · ·

AN OPUS TWO [a]

[*1831*]

Not long ago Eusebius stole quietly in through the door. You know the ironic smile on his pale face with which he seeks to arouse our expecta-tions. I was sitting at the piano with Florestan, who, as you know, is one of those rare men of music who foresee, as it were, all coming, novel, or extraordinary things. None the less there was a surprise in store for him

---

a This essay was published as early as 1831 in the *Allgemeine musikalische Zeitung*. As the one in which the Davidsbündler make their first appearance, it is given a place here also.

3 In addition to Schunke, Schumann's chief collaborators during the first year were Friedrich Wieck and Julius Knorr.

4 During its first year, the *Zeitschrift* described itself as "published by a society of artists and friends of art"; with the first number of the sec-ond volume this is changed to read "published under the direction of R. Schumann in association with a number of artists and friends of art."

5 An allusion to the title of Goethe's autobiog-raphy.

today. With the words "Hats off, gentlemen, a genius!" Eusebius placed
a piece of music on the stand. We were not allowed to see the title. I leafed
about absentmindedly among the pages; this veiled, silent enjoyment
of music has something magical about it. Furthermore, as it seems to me,
every composer has his own special way of arranging notes for the eye:
Beethoven looks different on paper from Mozart, very much as Jean
Paul's prose looks different from Goethe's. In this case, however, it was
as though unfamiliar eyes were everywhere gazing out at me strangely—
flower-eyes, basilisk-eyes, peacock-eyes, maiden-eyes; here and there
things grew clearer—I thought I saw Mozart's "Là ci darem la mano"
woven about with a hundred harmonies; Leporello seemed to be actually
winking at me, and Don Giovanni flew past me in a white cloak. "Now
play it!" Florestan suggested. Eusebius obeyed; huddled in a window
alcove, we listened. As though inspired, Eusebius played on, leading past
us countless figures from the realest of lives; it was as though the inspiration of the moment lifted his fingers above the usual measure of their
capabilities. Florestan's entire approval, except for a blissful smile, consisted, to be sure, in nothing but the remark that the variations might perhaps be by Beethoven or Schubert, had either of them been piano virtuosi
—but when he turned to the title page, read nothing more than:

Là ci darem la mano
varié pour le pianoforte par
Frédéric Chopin
Oeuvre 2

and both of us called out in amazement "An opus two!"—and when every
face glowed somewhat with more than usual astonishment and, aside from
a few exclamations, little was to be distinguished but: "At last, here's
something sensible again—Chopin—the name is new to me—who is he?—
in any case a genius—isn't that Zerlina laughing there or perhaps even
Leporello?"—then, indeed, arose a scene which I prefer not to describe.
Excited with wine, Chopin, and talking back and forth, we went off to
Master Raro, who laughed a great deal and showed little curiosity about
our Opus 2—"for I know you and your new-fangled enthusiasm too well
—just bring your Chopin here to me some time." We promised it for the
next day. Presently Eusebius bid us an indifferent good night; I remained
for a while with Master Raro; Florestan, who for some time had had no
lodgings, fled through the moonlit alley to my house. I found him in my
room at midnight, lying on the sofa, his eyes closed.

"Chopin's variations," he began, as though in a dream, "they are still
going around in my head. Surely the whole is dramatic and sufficiently

Chopinesque; the introduction, self-contained though it is—can you recall Leporello's leaping thirds?—seems to me to belong least of all to the rest; but the theme—why does he write it in B-flat?—the variations, the final movement, and the Adagio—these are really something—here genius crops up in every measure. Of course, dear Julius, the speaking parts are Don Giovanni, Zerlina, Leporello, and Masetto. In the theme, Zerlina's reply is drawn amorously enough. The first variation might perhaps be called somewhat elegant and coquettish—in it, the Spanish grandee toys aimiably with the peasant maid. This becomes self-evident in the second, which is already much more intimate, comic, and quarrelsome, exactly as though two lovers were chasing each other and laughing more than usual. But in the third—how everything is changed! This is pure moonshine and fairy spell—Masetto watches from afar and curses rather audibly, to be sure, but Don Giovanni is little disturbed. And now the fourth —what is your idea of it? Eusebius played it quite clearly—doesn't it jump about saucily and impudently as it approaches the man, although the Adagio (it seems natural to me that Chopin repeats the first part) is in B-flat minor, than which nothing could be more fitting, for it reproaches the Don, as though moralizing, with his misdeeds. It is bold, surely, and beautiful that Leporello listens, laughs, and mocks from behind the shrubbery, that the oboes and clarinets pour out seductive magic, and that the B-flat major, in full blossom, marks well the moment of the first kiss. Yet all of this is as nothing in comparison with the final movement—is there more wine, Julius?—this is Mozart's whole finale—popping corks and clinking bottles everywhere, in the midst of things Leporello's voice, then the grasping evil spirits in pursuit, the fleeing Don Giovanni—and finally the end, so beautifully soothing, so truly conclusive." Only in Switzerland, Florestan added, had he experienced anything similar to this ending; there, on a fine day, when the evening sun climbs higher and higher to the topmost peak where finally its last beam vanishes, there comes a moment in which one seems to see the white Alp-giants close their eyes. One feels only that one has seen a heavenly vision. "Now Julius, wake up, you too, to new dreams—and go to sleep!"

"Florestan of my heart," I answered, "these private feelings are perhaps praiseworthy, if somewhat subjective; but little as Chopin needs to think of listening to his genius, I still shall also bow my head before such genius, such aspiration, such mastery."

With that we fell asleep.

Julius.[6]

---

[6] This essay was Schumann's first published writing.

FLORESTAN'S SHROVE TUESDAY ADDRESS
DELIVERED AFTER A PERFORMANCE OF BEETHOVEN'S LAST SYMPHONY

[1835]

Florestan climbed on to the piano and spoke as follows:

Assembled Davidsbündler, that is, youths and men who are to slay the Philistines, musical and otherwise, especially the tallest ones (see the last numbers of the *Comet* [7] for 1833).

I am never overenthusiastic, best of friends! The truth is, I know the symphony better than I know myself. I shall not waste a word on it. After it, anything I could say would be as dull as ditch water, Davidsbündler. I have celebrated regular Ovidian Tristia, have heard anthropological lectures. One can scarcely be fanatical about some things, scarcely paint some satires with one's facial expression, scarcely—as Jean Paul's Giannozzo [8] did—sit low enough in the balloon for men not to believe that one concerns oneself about them, so far, far below do these two-legged creatures, which one calls men, file through the narrow pass, which one may in any case call life. To be sure, I was not at all annoyed by what little I heard. In the main I laughed at Eusebius. A regular clown, he flew impertinently at a fat neighbor who inquired confidentially during the Adagio: "Sir, did not Beethoven also write a battle symphony?" "Yes, that's the 'Pastoral' Symphony," our Euseb replied indifferently. "Quite right, so it is," the fat one expanded, resuming his meditations.

Men must deserve noses, otherwise God would not have provided them. They tolerate much, these audiences, and of this I could cite you magnificent examples; for instance, rascal, when at a concert you were turning the pages of one of Field's nocturnes for me. Unluckily, on one of the most broken-down rattle-boxes that was ever inflicted upon a company of listeners, instead of the pedal I stumbled on the Janizary stop [9]—piano enough, fortunately, so that I could yield to the impulse of the moment and, repeating the stroke softly from time to time, could let the audience believe some sort of march was being played in the distance. Of course Eusebius did his part by spreading the story; the audience, however, outdid themselves in applause.

Any number of similar anecdotes had occurred to me during the Adagio

---

[7] An "Unterhaltungsblatt" published in Altenburg from 1830 to 1836. In its issue for August 27, 1832, it had printed Schumann's "Reminiscences from Clara Wieck's Last Concerts in Leipzig."

[8] Principal character in Jean Paul's "Des Luft-

schiffers Giannozzo Seebuch," one of the humorous supplements to the second volume of his *Titan* (1801).

[9] A pedal producing the effect of bass drum and cymbals or triangle, much favored during the vogue of "Turkish music."

when we came to the first chord of the Finale. "What is it, Cantor," I said to a trembling fellow next to me, "but a triad with a suspended fifth, somewhat whimsically laid out, in that one does not know which to accept as the bass—the A of the kettledrum or the F of the bassoons? Just have a look at Türk, Section 19, page 7!" [10] "Sir, you speak very loud and are surely joking." With a small and terrifying voice I whispered in his ear: "Cantor, watch out for storms! The lightning sends ahead no liveried lackeys before it strikes; at the most there is first a storm and after it a thunderbolt. That's just its way." "All the same, such dissonances ought to be prepared." Just at that moment came the second one. "Cantor, the fine trumpet seventh shall excuse you." I was quite exhausted with my restraint—I should have soothed him with a sound blow.

Now you gave me a memorable moment, conductor, when you hit the tempo of the low theme in the basses so squarely on the line that I forgot much of my annoyance at the first movement, in which, despite the modest pretense of the direction "Un poco maestoso," there speaks the full, deliberate stride of godlike majesty.

"What do you suppose Beethoven meant by those basses?" "Sir," I replied gravely enough, "a genius often jests; it seems to be a sort of night-watchman's song." Gone was the exquisite moment, once again Satan was set loose. Then I remarked the Beethoven devotees—the way they stood there goggle-eyed, saying: "That's by our Beethoven. That's a German work. In the last movement there's a double fugue. Some reproach him for not excelling in this department, but how he has done it—yes, this is *our* Beethoven." Another choir chimed in with: "It seems as though all forms of poetry are combined in the work: in the first movement the epic, in the second the humorous, in the third the lyric, in the fourth—the blend of them all—the drama." Still another choir really applied itself to praising: "It's a gigantic work, colossal, comparable to the pyramids of Egypt." Still another went in for description: "The symphony tells the story of man's creation: first chaos, then the divine command 'Let there be light,' then the sun rising on the first man, who is delighted with such splendor—in short, it is the whole first chapter of the Pentateuch."

I became more frantic and more quiet. And while they were eagerly following the text and finally applauding, I seized Eusebius by the arm and pulled him down the brightly lighted stairs, smiling faces on either hand.

Below, in the darkness of the street lamps, Eusebius said, as though to himself: "Beethoven—what depths there are in the word, even the deep

10 D. G. Türk, *Kurze Anweisung zum Generalbassspielen* (Halle, 1791).

sonority of the syllables resounding as into an eternity! For this name, it is as though there could be no other characters." "Eusebius," I said with genuine calm, "do you too condescend to praise Beethoven? Like a lion, he would have raised himself up before you and have asked: 'Who, then, are you who presume this?' I do not address myself to you, Eusebius; you mean well—but must a great man then always have a thousand dwarfs in his train? They believe they understand him—who so aspired, who struggled against countless attacks—as they smile and clap their hands. Do those who are not accountable to me for the simplest musical rule have the effrontery to evaluate a master as a whole? Do these, all of whom I put to flight if I drop merely the word 'counterpoint'—do these who perhaps appreciate this and that at second hand and at once call out: 'Oh, this fits our corpus perfectly!'—do these who wish to talk of exceptions to rules they do not know—do these who prize in him, not the measure of his gigantic powers, but precisely the excess—shallow men of the world —wandering sorrows of Werther—overgrown, bragging boys—do these presume to love him, even praise him?"

Davidsbündler, at the moment I can think of no one so entitled but the provincial Silesian nobleman who recently wrote to a music dealer in this fashion:

Dear sir:

At last I have my music cabinet nearly in order. You ought to see how splendid it is. Alabaster columns on the inside, a mirror with silk curtains, busts of composers—in short, magnificent! In order, however, to give it a final touch of real elegance I ask you to send me, further, the complete works of Beethoven, *for I like this composer very much.*

What more there is that I should say, I should, in my opinion, scarcely know.

ENTHUSIASTIC LETTERS [b]

[*1835*]

1. Eusebius to Chiara

After each of our musical feasts for the soul there always reappears an angelic face which, down to the roguish line about the chin, more than

---

b These letters might also have been called "Wahrheit und Dichtung." They have to do with the first Gewandhaus concerts held under Mendelssohn's direction in October, 1835.

[The concerts in question were the first four in the subscription series; their dates were October 4, 11, 22, and 29. They are also covered in more conventional reviews published in the *Allgemeine musikalische Zeitung* for October 14 and 21 and for December 16, with the help of which it is possible to supply certain details passed over in Schumann's account.—Ed.]

resembles that of a certain Clara.[12] Why are you not with us, and how may you have thought last night of us Firlenzer, from the "Calm Sea" [13] to the resplendent ending of the Symphony in B-flat major? [14]

Except for a concert itself, I know of nothing finer than the hour before one, during which one hums ethereal melodies to oneself, the finger on the lips, walks up and down discreetly on one's toes, performs whole overtures on the windowpanes. . . . Just then it struck a quarter of. And now, with Florestan, I mounted the polished stairs.

"Seb," said he, "I look forward tonight to many things: first to the whole program itself, for which one thirsts after the dry summer; then to F. Meritis,[15] who for the first time marches into battle with his orchestra; then to the singer Maria,[16] with her vestal voice; finally to the public as a whole, expecting miracles—that public to which, as you know, I usually attach only too little importance." At the word "public" we stood before the old chatelain with his Commendatore face, who had much to do and finally let us in with an expression of annoyance, for as usual Florestan had forgotten his ticket. As I entered the brightly lighted golden hall I may, to judge from my face, have delivered perhaps the following address:

"With gentle tread I make my entrance, for I seem to see welling up here and there the faces of those unique ones to whom is given the fine art of uplifting and delighting hundreds in a single moment. There I see Mozart, stamping his feet to the symphony until a shoe-buckle flies off; there Hummel, the old master, improvising at the piano; there Catalani, pulling off her shawl, for the sound-absorbing carpet has been forgotten; there Weber; there Spohr; and many another. And there I thought also of you, my pure bright Chiara—of how at other times you spied down from your box with the lorgnette that so well becomes you." This train of thought was interrupted by the angry eye of Florestan, who stood, rooted to the spot, in his old corner by the door, and in his angry eye stood something like this:

"Think, Public, of my having you together again at last and of my being able to set you one against another . . . Long ago, overt ones, I wanted to establish concerts for deaf-mutes which might serve you as a pattern of how to behave at concerts, especially at the finest . . . Like Tsing-Sing,[17] you were to have been turned to a stone pagoda, had you

12 Quoted from an earlier letter to Clara (*Jugendbriefe* [Leipzig, 1885], p. 266). At the time of the writing of these letters, Clara Wieck was just sixteen.

13 Mendelssohn's overture.

14 Beethoven's "Fourth."

15 Mendelssohn.

16 Henriette Grabau.

17 A character in Auber's opera *Le Cheval de bronze* (1835).

dared to repeat anything of what you saw in music's magic realm," and so forth. The sudden deathlike silence of the public broke in on my reflections. F. Meritis came forward. A hundred hearts went out to him in that first moment.

Do you remember how, leaving Padua one evening, we went down the Brenta; how the tropical Italian night closed the eyes of one after another? And how, in the morning, a voice suddenly called out: "Ecco, ecco, signori —Venezia!"—and the sea lay spread out before us, calm and stupendous; how on the furthest horizon there sounded up and down a delicate tinkle, as though the little waves were speaking to one another in a dream? Behold—such is the wafting and weaving of the "Calm Sea"; [c] one actually grows drowsy from it and is rather thought than thinking. The Beethovenian chorus after Goethe [18] and the accentuated word sound almost raw in contrast to the spider's-web tone of the violins. Toward the end there occurs a single detached harmony—here perhaps a Nereid fixes the poet with her seductive glance, seeking to draw him under—then for the first time a wave beats higher, the sea grows by degrees more talkative, the sails flutter, the pennant leaps with joy, and now holloa, away, away, away. . . . Which overture of F. Meritis did I prefer, some artless person asked me; at once the tonalities E minor, B minor, and D major [19] entwined themselves as in a triad of the Graces and I could think of no answer better than the best—"Each one!" F. Meritis conducted as though he had composed the overture himself, and though the orchestra played accordingly, I was struck by Florestan's remarking that he himself had played rather in this style when he came from the provinces to Master Raro as an apprentice. "My most fatal crisis," he continued, "was this intermediate state between nature and art; always ardent as was my grasp, I had now to take everything slowly and precisely, for my technique was everywhere found wanting; presently there arose such a stumbling and stiffness that I began to doubt my talent; the crisis, fortunately, did not last long." I for my part was disturbed, in the overture as in the symphony, by the baton,[d] and I agreed with Florestan when he held that, in the symphony, the orchestra should stand there as a republic, acknowledging no superior. At the same time it was a joy to see F. Meritis and the way in which his eye anticipated every nuance in the music's intellectual windings, from the most delicate to the most powerful, and in which, as the most blissful one, he swam ahead of the rest, so different from those conductors

---

c The overture by Mendelssohn.
d Before Mendelssohn, in the days when Matthai was in charge, the orchestral works were performed without a conductor beating time.

18 Beethoven's Opus 112.
19 *A Midsummer Night's Dream, Fingal's Cave, Calm Sea and Happy Voyage.*

on whom one sometimes chances, who threaten with their scepter to beat score, orchestra, and public all in one.

You know how little patience I have with quarrels over tempi and how for me the movement's inner measure is the sole determinant. Thus the relatively fast Allegro that is cold sounds always more sluggish than the relatively slow one that is sanguine. In the orchestra it is also a question of quality—where this is relatively coarse and dense the orchestra can give to the detail and to the whole more emphasis and import; where this is relatively small and fine, as with our Firlenzer, one must help out the lack of resonance with driving tempi. In a word, the Scherzo of the symphony seemed to me too slow; one noticed this quite clearly also in the restlessness with which the orchestra sought to be at rest. Still, what is this to you in Milan—and, strictly speaking, how little it is to me, for I can after all imagine the Scherzo just as I want it whenever I please.

You asked whether Maria would find Firlenz as cordial as it used to be. How can you doubt it? Only she chose an aria which brought her more honor as an artist than applause as a virtuosa.[20] Then a Westphalian music director [21] played a violin concerto by Spohr [22]—good enough, but too lean and colorless.

In the choice of pieces, everyone professed to see a change in policy; if formerly, from the very beginning of the Firlenzer concerts, Italian butterflies fluttered about the German oaks, this time these last stood quite alone, as powerful as they were somber. One party sought to read in this a reaction; I take it rather for chance than for intention. All of us know how necessary it is to protect Germany from an invasion by your favorites; let this be done with foresight, however, and more by encouraging the youthful spirits in the Fatherland than by a needless defense against a force which, like a fashion, comes in and goes out.

Just at midnight Florestan came in with Jonathan, a new Davidsbündler, the two of them fencing furiously with one another over the aristocracy of mind and the republic of opinion. At last Florestan has found an opponent who gives him diamonds to crack. Of this mighty one you will hear more later on.

Enough for today. Do not forget to look in the calendar sometimes for August 13, where an Aurora links your name with mine.

Eusebius.

---

20 Weber's "Was sag ich? Schaudern macht mich der Gedanke!" for Cherubini's *Lodoiska*.

21 Otto Gerke.
22 No 11 in G major, Opus 70.

2. To Chiara

The letter carrier coming toward me blossomed out into a flower when I saw the shimmering red "Milano" on your letter. With delight I too recall my first visit to the Scala, just when Rubini was singing there with Méric-Lalande. For Italian music one must listen to in Italian company; German music one can enjoy under any sky.

I was quite right in not reading into the program of the last concert a reactionary intention, for the very next ones brought something Hesperidian. Whereat it was Florestan who amused me most; he finds this actually tiresome, and—out of mere irritation with those Handelians and other fanatics who talk as though they had themselves composed the Samson in their nightshirts—does not exactly attack the Hesperidian music, but compares it vaguely with "fruit salad," with "Titian flesh without spirit," and so forth, yet in so comical a tone that you could laugh out loud, did not his eagle eye bear down on you. "As a matter of fact," he said on one occasion, "to be annoyed with Italian things is long since out of fashion, and, in any case, why beat about with a club in this flowery fragrance which flies in and flies out? I should not know which world to choose—one full of nothing but refractory Beethovens or one full of dancing swans of Pesaro. Only two things puzzle me: our fair singers, who after all never know what to sing (excepting everything or nothing)— why do they never chance on something small, say, on a song by Weber, Schubert, Wiedebein; and then our German composers of vocal music, who complain that so little of their work reaches the concert hall—why do they never think of concert pieces, concert arias, concert scenas, and write something of this kind?"

The singer [23] (not Maria), who sang something from *Torvaldo*,[24] began her "Dove son? Chi m'aita?" in such a tremble that I responded inwardly: "In Firlenz, deary; aide-toi et le ciel t'aidera!" Presently, however, she showed her brighter side, the public its well-meant approval. "If only our German songbirds," Florestan interposed, "would not look on themselves as children who think one does not see them when they close their eyes; as it is, they usually hide themselves so stealthily behind their music that one pays the more attention to their faces and thus notices the difference between them and those Italian girls whom I saw singing at one another in the Academy at Milan with eyes rolling so wildly that I feared their artificial passion might burst into flames; this last I exag-

---

23 Fräulein Weinhold, from Amsterdam.   24 Rossini's *Torvaldo e Dorliska*.

gerate—still, I should like to read in German eyes something of the dramatic situation, something of the music's joy and grief; beautiful singing from a face of marble makes one doubtful of inner advantage; I mean this in a sort of general way."

Then you ought to have seen Meritis playing the Mendelssohn Concerto in G minor! Seating himself at the piano as innocently as a child, he now took captive one heart after another, drawing them along behind him in swarms, and, when he set you free, you knew only that you had flown past Grecian isles of the gods and had been set down again in the Firlenzer hall, safe and sound. "You are a very happy master in your art," said Florestan to Meritis when it was over, and both of them were right. Though my Florestan had spoken not a word to me about the concert, I caught him very neatly yesterday. To be precise, I saw him turning over the leaves of a book and noting something down. When he had gone, opposite this passage in his diary—"About some things in this world there is nothing to be said at all—for example, about Mozart's C major Symphony with the fugue, about many things in Shakespeare, about some things in Beethoven"—I read, written in the margin: "And about Meritis, when he plays the concerto by M."

We were highly delighted with an energetic overture of Weber's,[25] the mother of so many of those little fellows who tag along behind her, ditto with a violin concerto played by young ————,[26] for it does one good to be able to prophesy with conviction of a hard worker that his path will lead to mastery. With things repeated year in and year out—symphonies excepted—I shall not detain you. Your earlier comment on Onslow's Symphony in A [27]—that, having heard it twice, you knew it by heart, bar for bar—is also mine, although I do not know the real reason for this rapid commission to memory. On the one hand I see that the instruments still cling to one another too much and are piled on one another too heterogeneously; on the other hand the melodic threads—the principal and subsidiary ideas—come through so decidedly that, in view of the thick instrumental combination, their very prominence seems to me most strange. The principle ruling here is a mystery to me, and I cannot express it clearly. Perhaps it will stir you to reflection. I feel most at home in the elegant ballroom turmoil of the minuet, where everything sparkles with pearls and diamonds; in the trio I see a scene in an adjoining sitting room,

25 Either the Overture to the *Beherrscher der Geister*, played at the third concert on October 22, or that to *Euryanthe*, played at the fourth concert on October 29, probably the former.

26 Wilhelm Uhlrich, who played a concerto by L. W. Maurer.

27 No. 1, Opus 41, played at the fourth concert, on October 29.

into which, through the frequently opened ballroom doors, there penetrates the sound of violins, drowning out words of love. What do you
think?

This brings me very conveniently indeed to the A major Symphony
of Beethoven [28] which we heard not long ago. Moderately delighted, we
went, late in the evening as it was, to Master Raro. You know Florestan—
the way he sits at the piano and, while improvising, speaks, laughs, weeps,
gets up, sits down again, and so forth, as though in his sleep. Zilia sat in
the bay window, other Davidsbündler here and there in various groups.
There was much discussion. "I had to laugh"—thus Florestan began,
beginning at the same time the beginning of the symphony—"to laugh at
a dried-up notary who discovered in it a battle of Titans, with their
effectual destruction in the last movement, but who stole quietly past the
Allegretto because it did not fit in with his idea; to laugh in general at
those who talk endlessly of the innocence and absolute beauty of music in
itself—of course art should conceal, and not repeat, the unfortunate
octaves and fifths of life—of course I find, often in certain saintly arias (for
example, Marschner's), beauty without truth and, sometimes in Beethoven (but seldom), the latter without the former. But most of all my
fingers itch to get at those who maintain that Beethoven, in his symphonies, surrendered always to the grandest sentiments, the sublimest reflections, on God, immortality, and the cosmos, for if that gifted man does
point toward heaven with the branches of his flowering crown, he none
the less spreads out his roots in his beloved earth. To come to the symphony, the idea that follows is not mine at all, but rather someone's in
an old number of the *Cäcilia* [29] (the scene there changed—out of a perhaps exaggerated delicacy toward Beethoven which might well have been
spared—to the elegant hall of a count or some such place).

"It is the merriest of weddings, the bride a heavenly child with a rose
in her hair—but with one only. I am mistaken if the guests do not gather
in the introduction, do not greet one another profusedly with inverted
commas—very much mistaken if merry flutes do not remind us that the
whole village, with its Maypoles and their many-colored ribbons, takes
joy in Rosa, the bride—very much mistaken if the trembling glance of her
pale mother does not seem to ask: 'Dost not know that we must part?' and
if Rosa, quite overcome, does not throw herself into her mother's arms,
drawing the bridegroom after her with one hand. Now it grows very
quiet in the village outside (here Florestan entered the Allegretto, break-

---

28 Played at the third concert, on October 22.   29 A musical journal published in Mainz by
Schott, beginning in 1824.

ing off pieces here and there); only from time to time a butterfly floats by or a cherry blossom falls. The organ begins, the sun stands at its height, occasional long diagonal beams play through the church with bits of dust, the bells ring diligently, churchgoers gradually take their places, pews are opened and shut, some peasants look closely at their hymnbooks, others up into the choir loft, the procession draws nearer—at its head choir boys with lighted tapers and censers, then friends—often turning around to stare at the couple accompanied by the priest—then the parents and friends of the bride, with the assembled youth of the village bringing up the rear. How everything arranges itself, how the priest ascends to the altar, how he addresses, now the bride and now the fortunate one, how he speaks to them of the duties of the bond and of its purposes and of how they may find happiness in harmony and love of one another, how he then asks for her 'I do,' which assumes so much forever and forever, and how she pronounces it, firm and sustained—all this prevents my painting the picture further—do as you please with the finale"—thus Florestan broke off, tearing into the end of the Allegretto, and it sounded as though the sexton had so slammed the doors shut that the whole church re-echoed.

Enough. In me, too, Florestan's interpretation has stirred up something, and my alphabet begins to run together. There is much more for me to tell you, but the outdoors calls. Wait out the interval until my next letter with faith in a better beginning.

Eusebius.

DANCE LITERATURE

[1836]

J. C. Kessler:[30] Three Polonaises, Opus 25
Sigismund Thalberg:[31] Twelve Waltzes, Opus 4
Clara Wieck: Valses romantiques, Opus 4
Leopold, Edler von Meyer:[32] Salon (Six Waltzes), Opus 4
Franz Schubert: First Waltzes, Opus 9, Book 1
The same: Deutsche Tänze, Opus 33

"And now play, Zilia![33] I wish to duck myself quite under in the harmonies and only occasionally to poke out my head in order that you may not think me drowned from melancholy; for dance music makes one

---

[30] Joseph Christoph Kessler, concert pianist and composer for the piano, piano teacher in Lemberg, Warsaw, Breslau, and Vienna.
[31] Sigismund Thalberg, composer for the piano and concert pianist of the first rank, Liszt's chief rival, toured the United States in 1857 together with Vieuxtemps.

[32] Pupil of Czerny, concert pianist, toured the United States from 1845 to 1847 and again in 1867 and 1868.
[33] Clara Wieck.

sad and lax, just as church music, quite the other way, makes one joyful and active—me at least." Thus spake Florestan, as Zilia was already floating through the first Kessler polonaise. "Indeed it would be lovely," he continued, half-listening, half-speaking, "if a dozen lady-Davidsbündler were to make the evening memorable and would embrace each other in a festival of the Graces. Jean Paul has already remarked that girls ought really to dance only with girls (though this would lead, indeed, to there being some weddings fewer); men (I add) ought never to dance at all."

"Should they do so none the less," Eusebius interrupted, "when they come to the trio, he ought to say to his partner-Davidsbündler, 'How simple and how kind you are!' and, in the second part, it would be well if she were to drop her bouquet, to be picked up in flying past and rewarded with a grateful glance."

All this, however, was expressed more in Euseb's bearing and in the music than in anything he actually said. Florestan only tossed his head from time to time, especially at the third polonaise, most brilliant and filled with sounds of horn and violin.

"Now something livelier, and do you play the Thalberg, Euseb; Zilia's fingers are too delicate for it," said Florestan, who soon interrupted to ask that the sections be not repeated, since the waltzes were too transparent—particularly the ninth, which remained on one level, indeed on one measure—"and eternally tonic and dominant, dominant and tonic. Still, it's good enough for those whose ears are in their feet." But, at the end, the one who stood at the foot (a student) called out "Da capo!" in all seriousness, and everyone was obliged to laugh at Florestan's fury at this and at the way he shouted him down, telling him that he might be on his way, that he should interrupt with no further encouragements of this sort or he would silence him with an hour-long trill in thirds, and so forth.

"By a lady, then?" a reviewer might begin, seeing the *Valses romantiques*. "Well, well! Here we shan't need to hunt long for fifths and for the melody!"

Zilia held out four short moonlit harmonies. All listened intently. But on the piano there lay a sprig of roses—Florestan always had vases of flowers in place of the candelabras—and, shaken by the vibration, this had gradually slid down onto the keys. Reaching out for a note in the bass, Zilia struck against this too violently and left off playing, for her finger bled. Florestan asked what the matter was. "Nothing," said Zilia; "as in these waltzes, there is as yet no great pain, only a drop of blood charmed forth by roses." And may she who said this know no other.

A moment later, Florestan plunged into the midst of the brilliant countesses and ambassadresses of the Meyer *Salon.* How soothing this is —wealth and beauty, the height of rank and style, with music at the summit; every one speaks and no one listens, for the music drowns all out in waves! "For this," Florestan blurted out, "one really needs an instrument with an extra octave to the right and left, so that one can properly spread out and celebrate." You can have no idea of how Florestan plays this sort of thing and of how he storms away, carrying you along with him. The Davidsbündler, too, were quite worked up, calling in their excitement (musical excitement is insatiable) for "more and more," till Serpentin [34] suggested choosing between the Schubert waltzes and the Chopin boleros. "If, throwing myself at the keyboard from here," Florestan shouted, placing himself in a corner away from the piano, "I can hit the first chord of the last movement of the D minor symphony,[35] Schubert wins." He hit it, of course. Zilia played the waltzes by heart.

First waltzes by Franz Schubert: Tiny sprites, ye who hover no higher above the ground than, say, the height of a flower—to be sure, I don't care for the *Sehnsuchtswalzer,* in which a hundred girlish emotions have already bathed, or for the last three either, an aesthetic blemish on the whole for which I can't forgive the author—but the way in which the others turn about these, weaving them in, more or less, with fragrant threads, and the way in which there runs through all of them a so fanciful thoughtlessness that one becomes part of it oneself and believes at the last that one is still playing in the first—this is really first-rate.

In the *Deutsche Tänze,* on the other hand, there dances, to be sure, a whole carnival. " 'Twould be fine," Florestan shouted in Fritz Friedrich's [e] ear, "if you would get your magic lantern and follow the masquerade in shadows on the wall." Exit and re-enter the latter, jubilant.

The group that follows is one of the most charming. The room dimly lighted—Zilia at the piano, the wounding rose in her hair—Eusebius in his black velvet coat, leaning over her chair—Florestan (ditto), standing on the table and ciceronizing—Serpentin, his legs twined round Walt's [36] neck, sometimes riding back and forth—the painter à la Hamlet, parading

---

e The deaf painter. [The painter J. P. Lyser.—Ed.]

34 Carl Banck, music critic and composer of songs.

35 See above, p. 93.

86 The pianist Louis Rakemann, who emigrated to America in 1839.

his shadow figures through the bull's-eye, some spider-legged ones even running off the wall on to the ceiling. Zilia began, and Florestan may have spoken substantially to this effect, though at much greater length:

"No. 1. In A major. Masks milling about. Kettledrums. Trumpets. The lights go down. Perruquier: 'Everything seems to be going very well.' No. 2. Comic character, scratching himself behind the ears and continually calling out 'Pst, pst!' Exit. No. 3. Harlequin, arms akimbo. Out the door, head over heels. No. 4. Two stiff and elegant masks, dancing and scarcely speaking to one another. No. 5. Slim cavalier, chasing a mask: 'At last I've caught you, lovely zither player!' 'Let me go!' She escapes. No. 6. Hussar at attention, with plume and sabretache. No. 7. Two harvesters, waltzing together blissfully. He, softly: 'Is it thou?' They recognize each other. No. 8. Tenant farmer from the country, getting ready to dance. No. 9. The great doors swing open. Splendid procession of knights and noble ladies. No. 10. Spaniard to an Ursuline: 'Speak at least, since you may not love!' She: 'I would rather not speak, and be understood!' . . ."

But in the midst of the waltz Florestan sprang from the table and out the door. One was used to this in him. Zilia, too, soon left off, and the others scattered in one direction and another.

Florestan, you know, has a habit of often breaking off in the very moment when his enjoyment is at its height, perhaps in order to impress it in all its freshness and fullness on the memory. And this time he had his way—for whenever his friends speak to each other of their happiest evenings, they always recall the twenty-eighth of December, 18—— . . .

NEW PATHS

[*1853*]

Years have passed—nearly as many as I devoted to the former editorship of this journal, namely ten—since last I raised my voice within these covers, so rich in memories. Often, despite my intense creative activity, I have felt myself stimulated; many a new and signficant talent has appeared; a new musical force has seemed to be announcing itself—as has been made evident by many of the aspiring artists of recent years, even though their productions are chiefly familiar to a limited circle.[f] Following the paths of these chosen ones with the utmost interest, it has seemed to

---

f Here I have in mind Joseph Joachim, Ernst Naumann, Ludwig Norman, Woldemar Bargiel, Theodor Kirchner, Julius Schäffer, Albert Dietrich, not to forget that profoundly thoughtful student of the great in art, the sacred composer C. F. Wilsing. As their valiant advance guard I might also mention Niels Wilhelm Gade, C. F. Mangold, Robert Franz, and Stephen Heller.

me that, after such a preparation, there would and must suddenly appear some day one man who would be singled out to make articulate in an ideal way the highest expression of our time, one man who would bring us mastery, not as the result of a gradual development, but as Minerva, springing fully armed from the head of Cronus. And he is come, a young creature over whose cradle graces and heroes stood guard. His name is *Johannes Brahms,* and he comes from Hamburg where he has been working in silent obscurity, trained in the most difficult theses of his art by an excellent teacher who sends me enthusiastic reports of him,[g] recommended to me recently by a well-known and respected master. Even outwardly, he bore in his person all the marks that announce to us a chosen man. Seated at the piano, he at once discovered to us wondrous regions. We were drawn into a circle whose magic grew on us more and more. To this was added an altogether inspired style of playing which made of the piano an orchestra of lamenting and exultant voices. There were sonatas—veiled symphonies, rather; lieder, whose poetry one could understand without knowing the words, although a deep vocal melody ran through them all; single piano pieces, in part of a daemonic nature, most attractive in form; then sonatas for violin and piano; string quartets—and every work so distinct from any other that each seemed to flow from a different source. And then it seemed as though, roaring along like a river, he united them all as in a waterfall, bearing aloft a peaceful rainbow above the plunging waters below, surrounded at the shore by playful butterflies and borne along by the calls of nightingales.

Later, if he will wave with his magic wand to where massed forces, in the chorus and orchestra, lend their strength, there lie before us still more wondrous glimpses into the secrets of the spirit world. May the highest genius strengthen him for what expectation warrants, for there is also latent in him another genius—that of modesty. His comrades greet him on his first entrance into the world, where there await him wounds, perhaps, but also palms and laurels; we welcome him as a valiant warrior.

In every time, there reigns a secret league of kindred spirits. Tighten the circle, you who belong to it, in order that the truth in art may shine forth more and more brightly, everywhere spreading joy and peace.

R. S.

---

g Eduard Marxsen, in Hamburg.

9. Franz Liszt

On November 17, 1852, Berlioz's fourteen-year-old *Benvenuto Cellini*, which had not been heard since its dismal failure at the Opéra in 1838 and 1839, was brilliantly revived in Weimar under Liszt's direction. This was neither the first nor the last of Liszt's generous gestures in behalf of his old friend. Years earlier, in Paris, Liszt had been one of Berlioz's most zealous and most effective partisans. In February 1855 he was to arrange a second "Berlioz Week" in Weimar, and at this time the essay on Berlioz's *Harold,* an old project, began to take definite shape. A third series of concerts, in January 1856, led indirectly to the writing and composition of *Les Troyens.*

Since the publication of the collected letters of Liszt to Princess Caroline von Wittgenstein (1900–1902) and of the collected letters of Peter Cornelius (1904–1905), it has been generally recognized that Liszt was only in a very limited sense the author of the later writings published under his name. More recently, the publication of the memoirs of the Countess Marie d'Agoult (1927) and of her correspondence with Liszt (1933 and 1934) has made it clear that this is also true of the earlier writings. The *Lettres d'un bachelier-ès-musique* are largely the work of the Countess; the writings published from 1850 on—and these include the monographs on Wagner's *Tannhäuser* and *Lohengrin,* on Chopin, on Berlioz, and on the music of the gypsies—owe at least their literary form to the Princess. How much more they owe is not easy to say. Emile Haraszti ("Liszt—Author Despite Himself," *Musical Quarterly,* XXXIII, 490–516) does not hesitate to reduce Liszt's part in the collaboration to the vanishing point and to put the Princess in charge of "an editorial office that published under the name of Liszt" and whose output, except for the *Bohémiens,* is "without interest, either for Liszt's evolution or as literature." Surely this goes too far. That it was the Princess who first suggested the essay on Berlioz is clear from the published correspondence. But from this it is also clear that Liszt was to provide sketches for her to "develop." The correspondence shows further that Liszt spoke out when "developments" of this kind displeased him, that in the case of the essay on Berlioz he corrected a proof of the first installment, and that the Princess was obliged to consult him before she could cancel a trifling change that he had made in her wording of the title. Whether Haraszti is justified in calling the essay on Berlioz's *Harold* "obscure, idle balderdash," the reader may judge for himself. But if he agrees, Liszt must bear his share of the blame.

From Berlioz and His "Harold" Symphony [1]
[1855]

IN THE realm of ideas there are internal wars, like those of the Athenians, during which everyone is declared traitor to his fatherland who does not publicly take one side or the other and remains an idle spectator of the evil to which the struggle leads. Persuaded of the justice of this procedure, which, if rigorously observed, can only help to put an end to differences and to hasten the victory of those destined for future leadership, we have never concealed our lively and sympathetic admiration for the genius whom we intend to examine today, for the master to whom the art of our time is so decidedly indebted.

All the pros and cons of the noisy quarrel that has sprung up since the appearance of his first works can be reduced to one main point, to suggest which will suffice to show that the consequences inherent in his example go far beyond the pronouncements of those who consider themselves infallible arbitrators in these matters. The blunt antipathies, the accusations of musical high treason, the banishments for life which have been imposed on Berlioz since his first appearance—these have their explanation (why deceive ourselves about it?) in the holy horror, in the pious astonishment which came over musical authorities at the principle implicit in all his works, a principle that can be briefly stated in this form: *The artist may pursue the beautiful outside the rules of the school without fear that, as a result of this, it will elude him.* His opponents may assert that he has abandoned the ways of the old masters; this is easy—who wishes to persuade them of the contrary? His adherents may give themselves the greatest pains to prove that his way is neither always nor yet wholly and completely different from that to which one was formerly used; what do they gain thereby? Both parties remain convinced that Berlioz adheres no less firmly to the creed which we have just pronounced, whether this is demonstrated in fact by one or by one hundred corroborating circumstances. And for the authorities who have arrogated to themselves the privileges of

---

1 Text: *Neue Zeitschrift für Musik*, XLIII (1855), 25–26, 40–46, 49–55, 77–79, 80–81. The essay was published in five installments; the present abridged translation the beginning of the first installment, the latter part of the second, all of the third, and the beginning of the fourth.

As printed in 1855, the text is a translation into German, by Richard Pohl, from the French original of Liszt and the Princess Wittgenstein. The later German "translation," by Lina Ramann (*Gesammelte Schriften*, IV [Leipzig, 1882], 1–102) is simply a fussy revision of the earlier one.

orthodoxy this is a more than sufficient proof of his heresy. Yet since in art no sect maintains a dogma on the basis of revelation and only tradition is authoritative; since music in particular does not, like painting and sculpture, recognize or adhere to an absolute model; the deciding of disputes between orthodox and heresiarchs depends not only on the court of past and present science, but also on the sense for art and for the reasonable in the coming generation. Only after a considerable lapse of time can a final decision be handed down, for what verdict of the present will be acceptable on the one hand to the older generation,[a] which has borne from youth the easy yoke of habit, and on the other hand to the younger generation, who gather belligerently under any banner and love a fight for its own sake? Old and young must then entrust the solution of problems of this sort to a more or less distant future. To this future is alone reserved the complete or partial acceptance of those *violations of certain rules of art and habits of hearing* with which Berlioz is reproached. One point, however, is now already beyond all question. The representatives of the development to come will entertain a quite special respect for works exhibiting such enormous powers of conception and thought and will find themselves obliged to study them intensively, just as even now contemporaries approach them *nolens volens* step by step, their admiration only too often delayed by idle astonishment. Even though these works violate the rules, in that they destroy the hallowed frame which has devolved upon the symphony; even though they offend the ear, in that in the expression of their content they do not remain within the prescribed musical dikes; it will be none the less impossible to ignore them later on as one ignores them now, with the apparent intention of exempting oneself from tribute, from homage, toward a contemporary.

·   ·   ·   ·   ·

Heaven forbid that anyone, in holding forth on the utility, validity, and advantage of the program, should forswear the old faith and assert that the heavenly art does not exist for its own sake, is not self-sufficient, does not kindle of itself the divine spark, and has value only as the representative of an *idea* or as an exaltation of language. The choice between such an offense against the art and the complete renunciation of the pro-

---

a "The majority would like to see themselves benefited but do not wish their cherished ways of living disturbed, just as the sick man would gladly regain his health but gives up unwillingly that which has made him sick. . . . When an original work appears, demanding that the listener assimilate its ideas instead of appraising its new spirit in the light of traditional concepts and that he adopt the new concept absolutely essential to new ideas, the majority, in the midst of their fervent longings for the 'new,' shrink from the difficulty and find consolation in the warmed-over old, persuading themselves, wherever possible, that it is new."—Marx, *Die Musik des 19. Jahrhunderts* (2d ed., Leipzig, 1873), pp. 154–155.

gram cannot remain in doubt, and it would be better to allow one of its most prolific sources to dry up than, by denying its independent existence, to sever its vital nerve. Music embodies *feeling* without forcing it—as it is forced in its other manifestations, in most arts and especially in the art of words—to contend and combine with *thought*.[b] If music has one advantage over the other means through which man can reproduce the impressions of his soul, it owes this to its supreme capacity to make each inner impulse audible without the assistance of reason, so restricted in the diversity of its forms, capable, after all, only of confirming or describing our affections, not of communicating them directly in their full intensity, in that to accomplish this even approximately it is obliged to search for images and comparisons. Music, on the other hand, presents at one and the same time the intensity and the expression of *feeling;* it is the embodied and intelligible essence of feeling; capable of being apprehended by our senses, it permeates them like a dart, like a ray, like a dew, like a spirit, and fills our soul. If music calls itself the supreme art, if Christian spiritualism has transported it, as alone worthy of Heaven, into the celestial world, this supremacy lies in the pure flames of emotion that beat one against another from heart to heart without the aid of reflection, without having to wait on accident for the opportunity of self-assertion; it is breath from mouth to mouth, blood flowing in the arteries of life. Feeling itself lives and breathes in music without representational shell,[c] without the mediation of action or of thought; here it ceases to be cause, source, mainspring, moving and energizing principle, in order to reveal itself directly and without intercessory symbols in its indescribable totality, just

---

b "Music is spirit or soul, sounding without mediation for itself alone and finding satisfaction in its self-recognition; . . . the language of the soul, which pours out the inner joy and the sorrow of temperament in sound and in this outpouring raises itself in alleviation above natural emotional forces, in that it transforms the momentary state of affection in the inner self into one of self-recognition, into a free introspection, and in this way liberates the heart from oppression and suffering. . . . If now, speaking generally, we have already been able to regard activity in the realm of the beautiful as a liberation of the soul, as a renunciation of affliction and constraint, . . . then music carries this liberation to its extreme limit. . . . The special task of music is that, in presenting any content to the mind, it presents it neither as it is latent in consciousness as a general *concept,* nor as definite external *form* offers itself elsewhere to observation or is through art more completely represented, but rather in the way in which it becomes alive in the sphere of *subjective inwardness.*

". . . If we refrain from mere intellectual analysis and listen without restraint, the musical art work absorbs us completely and carries us along with it, independent of the power which art as art in general exerts on us. The peculiar power of music is an *elemental* power, that is to say, it lies wholly in the element of *sound* in which the art here moves."—Hegel, *Aesthetik*, III, iii, 2.

c "Let us readily concede that our art is incapable of immediately presenting a character picture or any other object clearly and completely to the eye, as do poetry and painting. As compensations, it transcends the latter in having the power of progressive development, the former in being able to present the simultaneous speech of distinct and contrary characters. It cannot call by name, cannot define who you are, but it can successively exhibit, as they become perceptible, all the impulses of your temperament. And it assembles you, with your likes and opposites, and presents you all to us just as you live, breathing and echoing out your lives, so that from the nature and being of the many we fully comprehend the one. It is a progressive monologue, filled to the full with a dialogue-like, dialectic content, two-sided and many-sided as Plato's dialogues aim to be, but treated artistically with the emphasis on genuinely dramatic contrasts and conflicts."—Marx, *loc. cit.*, p. 54.

as the God of the Christians, after having revealed Himself to the chosen through signs and miracles, now shows Himself to them through visions in the beatific aura of His substantial presence. Only in music does feeling, actually and radiantly present, lift the ban which oppresses our spirit with the sufferings of an evil earthly power and liberate us with the white-capped floods of its free and warmth-giving might from "the demon Thought," brushing away for brief moments his yoke from our furrowed brows. Only in music does feeling, in manifesting itself, dispense with the help of reason and its means of expression, so inadequate in comparison with its intuition, so incomplete in comparison with its strength, its deli-cacy, its brilliance. On the towering, sounding waves of music, feeling lifts us up to heights that lie beyond the atmosphere of our earth and shows us cloud landscapes and world archipelagos that move about in ethereal space like singing swans. On the wings of the infinite art it draws us with it to regions into which it alone can penetrate, where, in the ring-ing ether, the heart expands and, in anticipation, shares in an immaterial, incorporeal, spiritual life. What is it that, beyond this miserable, paltry, earthly shell, beyond these numbered planets, opens to us the meadows of infinity, refreshes us at the murmuring springs of delight, steeps us in the pearly dew of longing; what is it that causes ideals to shimmer be-fore us like the gilded spires of that submerged city, that recalls to us the indescribable recollections that surrounded our cradles, that conducts us through the reverberating workshops of the elements, that inspires us with all that ardor of thirsting after inexhaustible rapture which the bliss-ful experience; what is it that takes hold of us and sweeps us into the turbulent maelstrom of the passions which carries us out of the world into the harbor of a more beautiful life; is it not music, animated by elemental feeling like that which vibrates in us before it manifests itself, before it solidifies and turns cold in the mold of the idea? What other art discloses to its adepts similar raptures, the more precious and ennobling in that they are veiled by a chaste and impenetrable mystery? What other art reveals to its votaries the heavens where angels lovingly hold sway and flies with them in Elijah's chariot through spheres of ecstasy?

As the Slavic poet [2] has it: "The word belies the thought, the deed belies the word." Music does not belie feeling, it does not deceive it, and Jean Paul could exclaim: "O Music! Thou who bringest past and future so near our wounds with their flying flames! . . . O Music! Reverbera-tion from a distant world of harmony! Sigh of the angel within us! When the word is speechless, and the embrace, and the eye, and the tear; when

---

[2] Mickiewicz.

our dumb hearts lie lonely behind the ironwork of our breasts—then it is Thou alone through whom they call to one another in their dungeons and through whom, in their desert habitation, they unite their distant sighs!" [3] To Hoffmann, music revealed "that faraway country which surrounds us often with the strangest presentiments and from which wondrous voices call down to us, wakening all the echoes that sleep in our restricted breasts, which echoes, awakened now, shoot joyfully and gladly up, as though in fiery rays, making us sharers in the bliss of that paradise. . . . Is not music the mysterious language of a faraway spirit world whose wondrous accents, echoing within us, awaken us to a higher, more intensive life? All the passions battle with one another, their armor shimmering and sparkling, perishing in an inexpressible yearning which fills our breasts." [4]

·   ·   ·   ·   ·

Who has the temerity to deny to our inspired art the supreme power of self-sufficiency? But need making oneself master of a new form mean forever renouncing the hereditary and historically inculcated one? Does one forswear one's mother tongue when one acquires a new branch of eloquence? Because there are works that demand a simultaneous bringing into play of feeling and thought, shall on this account the pure instrumental style lose its magic for those works that prefer to expend themselves and their entire emotional wealth in music alone without being hindered by a definite object in their freedom of feeling? Would it not amount to a lack of confidence in the vitality of the pure instrumental style were one to anticipate its complete decay simply because there arose at its side a new species, distinct from drama, oratorio, and cantata, but having none the less in common with these the poetic basis?

The dwellers in the antipodes of this new artistic hemisphere will perhaps think to advance a telling argument against it by saying that program music, through its apparent reconciliation of various subspecies, surrenders its own individual character and may not for this reason lay claim to independent existence within the art. They will hold that our art attains its purest expression in instrumental music and that it has in this form arrived at its highest perfection and power, revealed itself in its most kingly majesty, and asserted its direct character most impressively; that music, on the other hand, has from time immemorial taken possession of the word with a view to lending it, through song, the charm and force of its expression and has in consequence always developed in two forms

---

as instrumental and vocal; that these two forms are equally indigenous, equally normal; and that the inventive creator, when he wishes to apply music to definite situations and actual persons, can find sufficient motives in the lyric and dramatic vocal forms; so that there can accordingly be no advantage or necessity for him to cause the peculiar properties of that form of music which exists for its own sake and lives its own life to meet and continue on the same path with the development of that other form which identifies itself with the poetic structure of the drama, with the sung and spoken word.

These objections would be well taken if in art two distinct forms could be *combined*, but not *united*. It is obvious that such a combination may be an unharmonious one, and that the work will then be misshapen and the awkward mixture offensive to good taste. This, however, will be due to a fault of execution, not a basic error. Are not the arts in general, and the several arts in particular, quite as rich in variously formed and dissimilar phenomena as nature is in the vicissitudes of her principal kingdoms and their divisions? Art, like nature, is made up of gradual transitions, which link together the remotest classes and the most dissimilar species and which are necessary and natural, hence also entitled to live.

Just as there are in nature no gaps, just as the human soul consists not alone in contrasts, so between the mountain peaks of art there yawn no steep abysses and in the wondrous chain of its great whole no ring is ever missing. In nature, in the human soul, and in art, the extremes, opposites, and high points are bound one to another by a continuous series of various varieties of *being*, in which modifications bring about differences and at the same time maintain similarities. The human soul, that middle ground between nature and art, finds prospects in nature which correspond to all the shadings and modulations of feeling which it experiences before it rests on the steep and solitary peaks of contradictory passions which it climbs only at rare intervals; these prospects found in nature it carries over into art. Art, like nature, weds related or contradictory forms and impressions corresponding to the affections of the human soul; these often arise from cross currents of diverse impulses which, now uniting, now opposing, bring about a divided condition in the soul which we can call neither pure sorrow nor pure joy, neither perfect love nor thorough egoism, neither complete relaxation nor positive energy, neither extreme satisfaction nor absolute despair, forming through such mixtures of various tonalities a harmony, an individuality, or an artistic species which does not stand entirely on its own feet, yet is at the same time different from any other. Art, regarded generally and in the position it occupies in

the history of mankind, would not only be impotent, it would remain incomplete, if, poorer and more dependent than nature, it were unable to
offer each movement of the human soul the sympathetic sound, the proper
shade of color, the indispensable form. Art and nature are so changeable in
their progeny that we can neither define nor predict their boundaries; both
comprise a host of heterogeneous or intimately related basic elements;
both consist in material, substance, and endlessly diverse forms, each of
them in turn conditioned by limits of expansion and force; both exercise
through the medium of our senses an influence on our souls that is as real
as it is indefinable.

An element, through contact with another, acquires new properties in
losing old ones; exercising another influence in an altered environment, it
adopts a new name. A change in the relative proportions of the mixture is
sufficient to make the resultant phenomenon a new one. The amalgama-
tion of forms distinct in their origins will result, in art as in nature, either
in phenomena of quite new beauty or in monstrosities, depending on
whether a harmonious *union* or a disagreeable *combination* promotes a
homogeneous whole or a distressing absurdity.

The more we persuade ourselves of the diverse unity which governs the
All in the midst of which man is situated and of that other unity which
rules his very life and history, the more we will recognize the diverse unity
which reveals itself in the destiny of art, the more we will seek to rid ourselves of our vicious inclination to carp at and curb it, like gardeners who
hem in the vegetation in order to grow hedges in a row or who cripple the
healthy tree for the sake of artificial shapes. Never do we find in *living*
natural phenomena geometrical or mathematical figures; why do we try
to impose them on art, why do we try to subject art to a rectilinear system?
Why do we not admire its luxurious, unfettered growth, as we admire the
oak, whose gnarled and tangled branches appeal in a more lively way to
our imaginations than does the yew, distorted into the shape of a pyramid
or mandarin's hat? Why all this desire to stunt and control natural and
artistic impulses? Vain effort! The first time the little garden-artist mis-
lays his shears, everything grows as it should and must.

Man stands in inverse relations to art and to nature; nature he rules as
its capstone, its final flower, its noblest creature; art he creates as a second
nature, so to speak, making of it, in relation to himself, that which he himself is to nature.[5] For all this, he can proceed, in creating art, only according to the laws which nature lays down for him, for it is from nature that
he takes the materials for his work, aiming to give them then a life supe-

---

[5] Cf. Richard Wagner, *Das Kunstwerk der Zukunft,* I (p. 136 below).

rior to that which, in nature's plan, would fall to their lot. These laws carry with them the ineradicable mark of their origin in the similarity they bear to the laws of nature, and consequently, for all that it is the creature of man, the fruit of his will, the expression of his feeling, the result of his reflection, art has none the less an existence not determined by man's intention, the successive phases of which follow a course independent of his deciding and predicting. It exists and flowers in various ways in conformity with basic conditions whose inner origin remains just as much hidden as does the force which holds the world in its course, and, like the world, it is impelled toward an unpredicted and unpredictable final goal in perpetual transformations that can be made subject to no external power. Assuredly, the scholarly investigator can follow up the traces of its past; he cannot, however, foresee the final purpose toward which future revolutions may direct it. The stars in the heavens come and go and the species inhabiting our earth appear and disappear in accordance with conditions which, in the fruitful and perpetual course of time, bring on and again remove the centuries. Thus it is also with art. The fecundating and life-giving suns of its realm gradually lose their brilliance and warmth, and there appear on its horizon new planets, proud, ardent, and radiant with youth. Whole arts die out, their former life in time recognizable only from the skeletons they leave behind, which, like those of antediluvian races, fill us with astonished surprise; through crossbreeding and blending new and hitherto unknown arts spring up, which, as a result of their expansion and intermingling, will perhaps someday be impelled toward their end, just as in the animal and vegetable kingdoms whole species have been replaced by others. Art, proceeding from man as he himself proceeds, it appears, from nature, man's masterpiece as he himself is nature's masterpiece, provided by man with thought and feeling—art cannot escape the inevitable change common to all that time begets. Coexistent with that of mankind, its life principle, like the life principle of nature, does not remain for long in possession of the same forms, going from one to another in an eternal cycle and driving man to create new forms in the same measure as he leaves faded and antiquated ones behind.

.   .   .   .   .

Like loving gifts of a nature infinitely exalted above his own, like traces within himself of elements that lie without him, man carries in his mind the concepts *eternity* and *nonexistence*. Kant first observed the enigmatic contradiction with which the mind, capable of grasping neither the one nor the other, accepts them both. These concepts constitute the two op-

posite poles of the axis about which man revolves, the idea of existence
without beginning or end, and that of nonexistence. Ceaselessly he circles
about these two points of reference, inclining now toward the one, now
toward the other, shrinking back from the thought of annihilation, horrified by the thought of the immutable. Man's whole environment is but
end and beginning, life after death and death before life. Nevertheless
he is seized instinctively and inexplicably with an aversion to the weak-
nesses of all beginnings, to the painful character of every end, while a
no less instinctive and inexplicable impulse urges him to destroy in order
to re-create. Experiencing disgust once he has reached the saturation point
and provoked to desire by his eagerness for novelty, he feels himself
impelled in perpetual alternation by an innate and sovereign longing for a
satisfaction to which he cannot give a name, but which every change seems
to promise him. From the struggle between these two exertions arise conflict and sorrow, our common, inevitable lot.

These two contradictory impulses, which suspend man's mind oscillat-
ing and fluctuating between permanence and instability, recur on every
hand: in the physical world as centripetal and centrifugal force, in chem-
istry as formation and disorganization, in morality as improvement and
deterioration, in politics as conservation and reform. A hidden power,
which we call providence or destiny, regulates their equilibrium by raising
or lowering the one scale or the other until, in unforeseen moments, it
brings them both into equal oscillation. Struck by the wondrous equilibrium of these so contradictory principles, an equilibrium wise beyond
comprehension, manifest in the destinies of mankind as in the worlds of
space, Newton exclaims: "Were centripetal and centrifugal forces equal,
they would destroy the cosmic mechanism; were they unequal, they would
engender chaos; God's finger must hold them in check!" In art and in its
oscillation between sterile, outworn forms which continue to vegetate,
bearing no new types, and the progress of evolving forms which are still
imperfect there is revealed *the finger of God* which Newton speaks of,
that mysterious impulse, that unseen law, which maintains harmony
among the most disparate elements, governing our progression in time
and beyond time through the agency of *genius*. Like the conquering
Gaul, it casts its shining sword into the scale of the attracting and repell-
ing forces which, on the one hand, draw art toward renewal, betterment,
and transformation, on the other seek to keep it in the old ruts, forms, and
modes of procedure. So long as genius fails to speak its magic word, this
dualism begets a more or less rapidly alternating ebb and flow, a deterioration or improvement of art and taste; sooner or later, however,

genius draws art past its laboriously surveyed boundaries in order that its beacon may light the way for mankind, striving forward, like our sun, toward a goal hidden from our sight, not comprehended by our reason. The sun, to be sure, pursues its course with even, measured steps toward that point of the firmament whose constellation has strangely and, as it were, prophetically been named for Hercules, for the liberator of the Prometheus in whom the human race is symbolized; mankind and art approach their supreme and final transfiguration irregularly and haltingly, now with the slowness and patience characteristic of the mole's subterranean labors, now with a powerful spring, such as the tiger takes toward his prey.

From this variety in the tempo of artistic development proceeds the difficulty of recognizing it in its portents and precursors. One must have taken a step forward before one can recognize as such the progress one has made. As long as this progress remains remote, like an anchorage toward which we sail, only a sort of clairvoyance will enable us to assert positively that we are getting ahead as we approach it. We border here so closely on optical illusion that for skeptics, who regard what others take for progress as retrogressive movement, there can be no demonstrations *a priori*. At the same time it would be idle to wish to deny or dispute an upward tendency in the psychological development of the human mind, which, embodying itself in constantly nobler arts and forms, strives after constantly wider radiation, after a brighter light, after an infinite exaltation.[d] And it would be equally idle to consign an art or the least of its forms to the class of immovable objects by seeking to demolish the new forms in which it manifests itself or to destroy the shoots that spring from the seeds

---

[d] "One cannot reflect on the deeper significance of the three great (so to speak) cardinal arts—plastics, painting, and music—without being constantly reminded of the history of the three great (so to speak) cardinal senses—touch, sight, and hearing. Then quite unsought there come to light most remarkable relations between the evolution of these senses in the animate world of the planets and the evolution of these forces in the history of mankind. Just as touch is the first and altogether most indispensable means by which the living creature orientates itself, so some form of plastics is the first and most essential art of peoples, the earliest to attain to full development. Sight, that miraculous perception of the most delicate light-effects, appears for the first time at a higher level in the animal kingdom, exhibiting, moreover, a certain inconstancy, seating itself now in a single eye, now in thousands of eyes, again on occasion degenerating altogether, even in the highest animal forms. The flowering of painting falls accordingly in mankind's middle period, assuming the most varied forms, coming to the fore and on occasion retreating suddenly into the background. Still later, indeed last of all, hearing develops, merely prefiguring itself in the higher mollusks and only from the fishes on becoming a permanent property of the animal world, seating itself now with greater constancy and symmetry in two organs, no more, no less, a right one and a left one, and from henceforth never again wanting. In similar measure, genuine music appears only in the last centuries; firm in its basic laws, at the same time developing itself and only holding to these as though riding at anchor, capable of the most delicate and most inspired variation, it thus becomes the mystery in which, free from all imitation of the world of actuality, the spiritualized world of feeling is reflected. If those other arts have long since passed the high point in their development, the full flowering of the tonal world falls in most recent times, and here, hidden under a thin shell, there are still latent many secrets, ready assuredly to reveal themselves to the right rhabdomancer."—Carus.

of ripened fruit. These can never be stunted; no profane hand can restrain their seasonal impulse.

Strange contradiction! Nothing human stands still; cult, custom, law, government, science, taste, and mode of enjoyment—all change, all are constantly coming and passing away, without rest, without respite; no country is quite like any other, and no century ends in the same atmosphere with which it began; the endeavors, tendencies, improvements, and ideals of each generation plow up the hereditary fields in order to experiment with a new kind of crop. Yet in the midst of all these ferments, in this tempest of time, in this eternal world-rejuvenation, resembling the transformations of nature, if not in majesty then at least in universality, among all the paths of progress is one alone to remain untrodden —among all the manifestations of the human spirit is the development of the purest and most brilliant one to be forbidden, its mobility forever held in check? Among all the virtual forces, is it proposed to deny precisely to this force, to the supreme force, the possibility of perfection that spirit inspires in matter, which possibility, an echo of that first command of creation, forms, with its "Become!", a harmonious All from the reorganized elements of an embryonic chaos? Wondrous power, noblest sacred gift of existence! Where else but in art canst thou be found? However man employs himself on any path of life, however he discovers, invents, collects, analyzes, and combines—he *creates* only in the art work; only here can he out of free will embody feeling and thought in a sensual mold that will preserve and communicate their sense and content. Is art alone, from a given moment on, to remain unaffected by the ebb and flow of its soul, unmoved by the fluctuations of its hopes, unresponsive to all the changing of its dreams, to all the budding and weaving of its ideas? No, certainly not! Art, in general and in particular, sails with mankind down the stream of life, never to mount again to its source. Even when it appears to stand still momentarily, the tides which bear man and his life continue to remain its element. Art moves, strides on, increases and develops, obeying unknown laws, in cycles whose dissimilar return, recurring like the appearance of certain comets, at unpredictable intervals, does not permit the positive assertion that they will not again pass overhead in all their splendor or having passed will not return once more. Only it is not given us to foresee its unawaited reappearance or the undreamed-of glory in which it will then come forward.

· · · · ·

When the hour of progress strikes for art, the genius is always found in the breach; he fulfills the need of the times, whether it be to bring a discovery from out a misty limbo fully and completely into the light or whether it be to combine single syllables, childishly strung together, into a sonorous word of magical power. It sometimes happens that art blossoms like the plant which gradually unfolds its leaves and that its successive representatives complement one another in equal proportion, so that each master takes only a single step beyond what his teacher has transmitted to him. In such cases, the masses, to whom this slow progress allows ample time, whose *niveau* is only gradually elevated, are enabled to follow the quest for more perfect procedures and higher inspiration. In other cases, the genius leaps ahead of his time and climbs, with one powerful swing, several rungs of the mystic ladder. Then time must elapse until, struggling after him, the general intellectual consciousness attains his point of view; before this happens it is not understood and cannot be judged. In literature, as also in music, this has often been the case. Neither Shakespeare nor Milton, neither Cervantes nor Camoëns, neither Dante nor Tasso, neither Bach nor Mozart, neither Gluck nor Beethoven (to cite only these glorious names) was recognized by his own time in such measure as he was later. In music, which is perpetually in a formative state (and which in our time, developing at a rapid tempo, no sooner accomplishes the ascent of one peak than it begins to climb another), the peculiarity of the genius is that he enriches the art with unused materials as well as with original manipulations of traditional ones, and one can say of music that examples of artists who have, as it were, leaped with both feet into a future time, are here to be found in greatest abundance. How could their anticipation of the style which they recognized as destined for supremacy fail to be offensive to their contemporaries, who had not sufficient strength to tear themselves loose, as they had done, from the comfortable familiarity of traditional forms? Yet, though the crowd turn its back on them, though envious rivals revile them, though pupils desert them, though, depreciated by the stupid and damned by the ignorant, they lead a tortured, hunted life, at death they leave behind their works, like a salutary blessing. These prophetic works transmit their style and their beauty to one after another of those who follow. It often happens that talents little capable of recognizing their significance are the very first to find ways of utilizing certain of their poetic intentions or technical procedures, whose value they estimate according to their lights. These are soon imitated again and thus forced to approach more closely to what was at first misunderstood, until, in the fumbling inherent in such imitations and tentative approaches, there is finally attained the understanding and glorification of the genius who, in his lifetime, demanded recognition in vain. Not until it has become used to admiring works analogous to his, but of lesser value, does the public receive his precious bequest with complete respect and jubilant applause. The old forms, thus made obscure, soon fall into neglect and are finally forgotten by the younger generation that has grown up with the new ones and finds these more acceptable to its poetic ideal. In this way the gap between the genius, gifted with wings, and the public which follows him, snail-like and circumspect, is gradually filled out.

.   .   .   .   .

The poetic solution of instrumental music contained in the program seems to us rather one of the various steps forward which the art has still to take, a necessary result of the development of our time, than a symptom of its exhaustion and decadence, for we cannot presume that it is now already obliged to resign itself to the subtleties and aberrations of *raffinement* in order that, after having drained all its auxiliary sources and worn out all its means, it may cover up the impotence of its declining years. If hitherto unused forms arise and, through the magic they exert, win acceptance for themselves with thoughtful artists and with the public, in that the former makes use of them while the latter shows its receptivity toward them, it is not easy to demonstrate their advantages and inconveniences in advance so exhaustively that one can strike an average on the basis of which to establish their expectation of longevity and the nature of their future influence. None the less it would be petty and uncharitable to abstain from inquiry into their origin, significance, bearing, and aim in order to treat works of genius with a disdain of which one may later have reason to be ashamed, in order to withhold due recognition to a widening of the field of art, stamping it, on the contrary and without further ado, as the excrescence of a degenerate period.

We shall forgo deriving advantage from a pronouncement of Hegel's if we can be convinced that great minds (those before whose Herculean intellectual labors every head is bowed, quite apart from sympathy for their doctrines) can characterize precisely those forms as desirable which reveal themselves as sickly and contributory to the downfall of art. Hegel appears to foresee the stimulation which the program can give to instrumental music by increasing the number of those understanding and enjoying it when he says, at the end of the chapter on music in his *Aesthetics*, the intuitive correctness of which as a general survey cannot be prejudiced by certain erroneous conceptions, such as its time brought with it:

The connoisseur, to whom the inner relationships of sounds and instruments are accessible, enjoys in instrumental music its artistic use of harmonies, interwoven melodies, and changing forms; he is wholly absorbed by the music itself and takes a further interest in comparing what he hears with the rules and precepts which he knows in order to appraise and enjoy the accomplishment to the full, though here the ingenuity of the artist in inventing the new can often embarrass even the connoisseur, to whom precisely this or that progression, transition, etc., is unfamiliar. So complete an absorption is seldom the privilege of the amateur, to whom there comes at once a desire to fill out this apparently meaningless outpour of sound and to find intellectual footholds for its progress and, in general, more definite ideas and a more precise content for that which penetrates into his soul. In this respect, music becomes symbolic for him, yet, in his attempts to overtake its meaning, he is confronted by abstruse problems, rapidly rushing by, which do not always lend themselves to solution and which are altogether capable of the most varied interpretations.

We would modify Hegel's opinion only to state it in a more absolute form, for we cannot concede that the *artist* is satisfied with forms that are too dry for the *amateur*. We assert, on the contrary, that the artist, even more insistently than the amateur, must demand emotional content in the formal container. Only when it is filled with the former does the latter have significance for him. The artist and the connoisseur who, in creating and judging, seek only the ingenious construction, the artfully woven pattern, the complex workmanship, the *kaleidoscopic* multiplicity of mathematical calculation and intertwining lines, drive music toward the dead letter and are to be compared with those who look at the luxuriant poetry of India and Persia only from the point of view of grammar and language, who admire only sonority and symmetrical versification, and do not regard the meaning and wealth of thought and image in its expression, its poetic continuity, not to mention the subject which it celebrates or its historical content. We do not deny the usefulness of philological and geological investigations, chemical analyses, grammatical commentaries—but they are the affair of science, not of art. Every art is the delicate blossom which the solid tree of a science bears at the tips of its leafy branches; the roots ought to remain hidden by a concealing coverlet. The necessity and utility of separating the material and substance in which art embodies itself into their component parts with a view to learning to know and to use their properties do not justify the confusing of science and art, of the study of the one with the practice of the other. Man must investigate art and nature; this is however not the goal of his relation to them—it is essentially a preparatory—if likewise important—moment in them. Both are given him primarily for his *enjoyment;* he is to absorb the divine harmonies of nature, to breathe out in art the melodies of his heart and the sighs of his soul. A work which offers only clever manipulation of its materials will always lay claim to the interest of the immediately concerned—of the artist, student, and connoisseur—but, despite this, it will be unable to cross the threshold of the artistic kingdom. Without carrying in itself the divine spark, without being a living poem, it will be ignored by society as though it did not exist at all, and no people will ever accept it as a leaf in the breviary of the cult of the beautiful. It will retain its value only as long as the art remains in a given state; as soon as art moves on to a new horizon and through experience learns improved methods, it will lose all significance save the historic and will be filed away among the archaeological documents of the past. Poetic art works, on the other hand, live for all time and survive all formal revolution, thanks to the indestructible life principle which the human soul has embodied in them.

If instrumental music calls itself the summit of our art, its least constrained and most absolute manifestation, it does so either by virtue of its capacity to give to certain feelings and passions an expression intelligible to the listener, affecting his soul while his mind follows a logical development agreeing with his inner one, or by virtue of the indescribable enjoyment of indefinable impressions which, by force or in alleviation, transform our whole being into a state, incomprehensible to the unresponsive, often called contemplation of the ideal, so aptly characterized by Hegel as a sort of *liberation of the soul,* since the soul actually believes itself released from all material fetters and resigns itself unhampered to emotion's endless sea. Each musical constitution recounts to itself, if not quite clearly then at least in an approximate way, the impression which an instrumental poem should transmit from the author to the listener and is conscious of the passions and feelings and their modifications which it unfolds. Even though, in accordance with the propensity of his imagination, the individual clothes these passions and feelings with images of his own, he will be unable to deceive himself about the sort of temperamental activity which the composer intended his work to evoke. Assuredly, one cannot judge a musician's character better than by defining the mood which he leaves in the listener. The difference between the tone-poet and the mere musician is that the former reproduces his impressions and the adventures of his soul in order to communicate them, while the latter

manipulates, groups, and connects the tones according to certain established rules and, thus playfully conquering difficulties, attains at best to
novel, bold, unusual, and complex combinations.[e] Yet, since he speaks to
men neither of his joys nor of his sorrows, neither of resignation nor of
desire, he remains an object of indifference to the masses and interests
only those colleagues competent to appreciate his facility. The rest pronounce on him the most deadly sentence of all—they call him *dry*, meaning thereby that there flows in his work no vital sap, no noble blood, no
burning passion, that it is a mere aggregation or crystallization of un-
organic particles, comparable to those which scientists exclude from the
science of life (biology), that is, from the realm of the living. But still—
strange paradox—it is only the *tone-poet* who can widen the boundaries
of the art by breaking the chains which restrain the free soaring of his
fantasy. Only

> The Master can the moment choose
> With skillful hand to break the mold.[f]

---

[e] May we be permitted to quote once again from Hegel, who, in his appraisal and presentation of many important points in music, was led on by that keenness of instinct, often met with in talented constitutions, which deceives them less often than sophistry does in matters which they are incapable of regarding with the same impartiality.

"It may be, on the one hand, that we enjoy mere sensuous sound and euphony without further inward participation; on the other hand, that we follow the harmonic and melodic succession which neither affects nor extends the inner self, observing it intellectually. Such a purely intellectual analysis, for which there is nothing in the art work beyond the ingenuity of skillful fabrication, is indeed present in music to an unusual degree. . . . To be sure, the composer can impart to his work a certain meaning, a content of ideas and emotions in organized and self-contained succession; conversely, without regard for such a content, he can concern himself with the purely musical structure of his work and with the ingenuities of such architectonic. In this case, however, the musical product can easily become something relatively devoid of thought and feeling, requiring otherwise no deep consciousness, cultivation, or temperament. As a result of this want of matter, we can frequently observe the development of the gift of composition in very young children, and talented composers often go through life the most inane and unobservant of men. The deeper implication, then, is that even in instrumental music the composer should devote equal attention to both sides—to the expression of an admittedly indefinite content and to musical structure—whereby he is once more at liberty to give the preference now to the melodic, now to the depth and complexity of the harmonic, now to the characteristic, and also to combine these elements one with another. . . . I have already observed that of all the arts, music possesses the greatest capacity for freeing itself, not only from any actual text, but also from the expression of any definite content, finding satisfaction in a mere self-contained succession of the combinations, modifications, contrasts, and transitions that fall within the province of the purely musical. Then, however, music remains empty and meaningless, and, lacking one of the chief sides of art in general, is not yet properly to be reckoned as art. Only when a spiritual content is adequately expressed in the sensual element of the sounds and their varied configurations does music rise to the level of genuine art, regardless of whether this content receives its more immediate identification expressly through words or whether it is in a less definite way perceptible in the sounds and their harmonic relationships and melodic animation."

For all that Hegel is criticized for having spoken about music without possessing a wide knowledge of the art, we find his judgments on the whole to the point, as though dictated by that straightforward, healthy intelligence which coincides with the general conviction. He furthermore admits his lack of competence with a modesty which less important folk would do well to imitate and complains that his requests to be set right met with little response. "The sound and exhaustive treatment of the subject," he says, "presupposes a more exact knowledge of the rules of composition and a wholly different acquaintance with the masterpieces of musical literature than I possess or have been able to obtain at second hand, for one never hears anything detailed or definite about these matters from connoisseurs and practical musicians as such, from the latter, often the most unintelligent of people, least of all."

[f] Schiller, *Das Lied von der Glocke* (translated by J. S. Dwight, Boston, 1839).

The specifically musical composer, who attaches importance to the consumption of the material alone, is not capable of deriving new forms from it, of breathing into it new strength, for no intellectual necessity urges him —nor does any burning passion, demanding to be revealed, oblige him— to discover new means. To enrich the form, to enlarge it and make it serviceable, is granted, then, precisely to those who make use of it only as one of the means of expression, as one of the languages which they employ in accordance with the dictates of the ideas to be expressed; the formalists can do nothing better or more intelligent than to use, to popularize, to subdivide, and on occasion to rework what the tone-poets have won.

The program asks only acknowledgment for the possibility of precise definition of the psychological moment which prompts the composer to create his work and of the thought to which he gives outward form. If it is on the one hand childish, idle, sometimes even mistaken, to outline programs after the event, and thus to dispel the magic, to profane the feeling, and to tear to pieces with words the soul's most delicate web, in an attempt to *explain* the feeling of an instrumental poem which took this shape precisely because its content could not be expressed in words, images, and ideas; so on the other hand the master is also master of his work and can create it under the influence of definite impressions which he wishes to bring to full and complete realization in the listener. The specifically musical symphonist carries his listeners with him into ideal regions, whose shaping and ornamenting he relinquishes to their individual imaginations; in such cases it is extremely dangerous to wish to impose on one's neighbor the same scenes or successions of ideas into which our imagination feels itself transported. The painter-symphonist, however, setting himself the task of reproducing with equal clarity a picture clearly present in his mind, of developing a series of emotional states which are unequivocally and definitely latent in his consciousness—why may he not, through a program, strive to make himself fully intelligible?

· · · · ·

If music is not on the decline, if its rapid progress since Palestrina and the brilliant development which has fallen to its lot since the end of the last century are not the preordained limits of its course, then it seems to us probable that the programmatic symphony is destined to gain firm footing in the present art period and to attain an importance comparable to that of the oratorio and cantata—in many respects to realize in a modern sense the meaning of these two species. Since the time when many masters brought the oratorio and cantata style to its highest brilliance, to its final perfection, its successful treatment has become difficult; for other reasons too, whose discussion would here be out of place, the two species no longer arouse the same interest as at the time when Handel animated them with the breath of the winged steer. Oratorio and cantata appear to resemble drama in their impersonation and dialogue. But these are after all external similarities, and close examination reveals at once that undeniable differences of constitution prevail. Conflicts of passions, delineations of characters, unexpected peripetias, and continuous action are in them even more noticeably absent than actual representation; indeed we do not for one moment hesitate to deny a close relation here and are on the contrary persuaded that in this form music approaches rather the antique *epos*, whose essential features it can thus best reproduce. Aside from dialogue, held together by a certain continuity in the action it presents, oratorio and cantata have no more in common with the stage than has the epos; through their leaning toward the descriptive, instrumentation lends them a similar frame. Episode and apostrophe play almost the same role in them, and the effect of the whole is that of the solemn recital of a memorable event, the glory of which falls undivided on the head of a single hero. If we were asked which musical form corresponded most closely to the poetic epos, we should doubt whether better examples could be brought forward than the *Israel, Samson, Judas Maccabaeus, Messiah*, and *Alexander* of Handel, the Passion of Bach, the *Creation* of Haydn, the *St. Paul* and *Elijah* of Mendelssohn.

The program can lend to instrumental music characteristics corresponding almost exactly to the various poetic forms; it can give it the character of the ode, of the dithyramb, of the elegy, in a word, of any form of lyric poetry. If all along it has been expressing the moods proper to these various species, it can by defining its subject draw new and undreamed-of advantages from the approximation of certain ideas, the affinity of certain figures, the separation or combination, juxtaposition or fusion of certain poetic images and perorations. What is more, the program can make feasible for music the equivalent of a kind of poetry unknown to antiquity and owing its existence to a characteristically modern way of feeling—the poem ordinarily written in dialogue form which adapts itself even less readily than the epos to dramatic performance.

It is our opinion that one does violence to the stage, to say the least, when one seeks to impose constructions on it that have taken root and flowered in other fields of poetry and literature and have gone through a development quite different from its own. For all this, the stage is always more receptive to the transplanting of motives from the classical epos than it is to those modern poems which, for want of a better name, we shall call *philosophical epopoeias;* among these Goethe's *Faust* is the colossus, while beside it Byron's *Cain* and *Manfred,* and the *Dziady* of Mickiewicz constitute immortal types. In the epos it is not the persons, but the action, that is unsuited to the theater; the genius, however, can overcome this difficulty, if not without effort, then the more brilliantly. In the epopoeia it is the persons themselves who fail to meet the requirements of the stage, for they are for the most part animated by feelings which, in their height and depth, are inaccessible to the majority who make up the bulk of the dramatic audience.

In the epos and in Homer, its inspired model, it is a hero, gifted with heroic human virtues, whose great deeds occupy the foreground, while a series of the figures of episodic narrative group themselves about him. Their great number is regarded as an enrichment of the work, the variety of their several appearances as one of its beauties. They are depicted with quick, bold strokes and exhibit their characters through actions and speeches without precise description or detailed portrayal. The play of their simple, natural passions is content with the presumptions granted by ordinary experience. The marvelous appears here as something quite as foreign and superior to man's will as natural force. Nature herself is depicted in her full coloring and admired as a power, as a drama. In the modern epopoeia she is rather celebrated than depicted; here her mysterious relations to the constitution of the human soul are unriddled; here she almost ceases to be an object and intervenes in the development as though an active person, in order to curb man by her example, sharing his impressions, consoling him, and lulling him to sleep with her dreams. Before her, the action and the event lose their importance, and the number of the episodic figures, apart from this sketched only lightly, shrinks together. The marvelous gives place to the fantastic; wholly exempt from the laws of probability, compressed and modified, the action acquires a symbolic luster, a mythological basis. No longer do supernatural beings disturb us by their intrusion into the development of human interests; they have to a certain extent become embodiments of passionate desires and hopes and appear now as personifications of our inner impulses. No longer does the poem aim to recount the exploits of the principal figure; it deals with affections active within his very soul. It has become far more important to show what the hero thinks than how he acts, and for this reason a limited concurrence of facts suffices to demonstrate how predominantly this or that feeling affects him. Dialogue becomes of necessity an excuse for monologue. To be sure, a hero is still celebrated, not however with a view to recalling his wanderings, for not even the choice of hero falls any longer on those who are patterns of extraordinary virtues. On the contrary, the modern hero often typifies rare and abnormal impulses, little familiar to the human heart. How these take root in the soul, mount flaming to the heavens, and, in subsiding, cast a flickering light on the ruins of the heart—all this is painstakingly and exhaustively depicted. While the antique epos exhibits to us the majority of mankind and, in its truthful and exact portrayal of character, causes us to admire its profound insight into the soul, the romantic species, as we shall call it, seeks out exceptional figures only; these it draws far beyond life-size and in unusual situations, so that there recognize themselves in them only those constitutions that are formed of a finer clay and animated by a warmer breath, that lead a more powerfully pulsating life than others, with a more responsive soul. Nevertheless they often exert an irresistible magic for all, idealizing in the eye of the plain man inclinations which he experiences and understands in a similar way, only more dully, less distinctly, less pervasively. The supreme charm and greatest merit of these art works lie in their eloquent expression of the most animated, most profound, and often most penitent feelings of great hearts.

If now, despite essential differences, we identify these two species of poetry and group them together under the common name *epopoeia*, we do so because of a similarity which seems to us more important than that of form and scale. Thanks to the cast which genius has given to their features, both species—small in number but great in value—reflect in the most lively manner the spirit of the age and nation which produced them. The antique epos offers us a typical, almost statuesque picture of ancient peoples. Formerly, in the poet's work, a people recognized themselves, as in a faithful mirror, with their morals, their religion, their politics, and their whole activity; today, however, when the distinguishing features of those peoples participating in the Christian civilization tend more and more to become obliterated, the poet naturally feels more drawn to characterize the century and the way of feeling which animates the man of the century (as Goethe and Byron have done in figures whose nationality one recognizes, so to speak, only from their costumes), to give permanent form to the ideal psychological impulse which in his time animates the cultivated man throughout Europe. Why should not music join in this new manifestation of the human spirit?

In literature, no one any longer denies that Goethe and Byron were justified in inventing or introducing the *philosophical epopoeia* as a narrative of inner events, of the fermentation, within the heart, of germs predominantly present in this or that nation or epoch, of exclusive psychological states which, when transferred to an individual being, impel it to actions sufficient to sign a destiny with the stamp of evil. No one any longer complains that these great poets chose as heroes exceptional natures, comparable to those legendary wonder-plants whose blossoms, responsive to the favorable or pernicious external conditions of their existence, distilled a corrosive poison, so that they either destroyed themselves or became fruits of paradise from which a single drop of ambrosia could reanimate the most withered lips. Is music unsuited to cause such natures to speak its language? To represent their origin and metamorphosis, their glorious ascent or downfall, their morbid outbreaks and redeeming powers, to portray their inspiring or awesome end? But could music do this in the drama? Scarcely. Literature itself cannot present upon the stage passions whose meandrine progress must be followed from their source to their disappearance in the eddies of the past. The interest which they arouse attaches itself far more to inner events than to actions related to the outer world.

Would perhaps the specifically musical symphony be better suited to such subjects? We doubt it. The conflict between its independent style and the one forced on it by the subject would affect us disagreeably, being without evident or intelligible cause. The composer would cease to conduct our imagination into the regions of an ideal common to all mankind and, without definitely announcing the particular path he wishes to choose, would only lead the listener astray. With the help of a program, however, he indicates the direction of his ideas, the point of view from which he grasps a given subject. The function of the program then becomes indispensable, and its entrance into the highest spheres of art appears justified. Surely we have no wish to question the capacity of music to represent characters similar to those the poet princes of our time have drawn. For the rest, we see music arrived at such a point in its relations of dependence on and correspondence with literature, we see at the same time all human feeling and thinking, aim and endeavor, so overwhelmingly directed toward profound inquiry into the sources of our sufferings and errors, we see all other arts, vying one with another in their efforts to satisfy the taste and needs of our time, consumed so specifically by the desire to give expression to this urge, that we consider the introduction of the program into the concert hall to be just as inevitable as the declamatory style is to the opera. Despite all handicaps and setbacks, these two trends will prove their strength in the triumphant course of their development. They are imperative necessities of a moment in our social life, in our ethical training, and as such will sooner or later clear a path for themselves. The custom of providing instrumental pieces with a program has already found such acceptance with the public that musicians cease to struggle against it, regarding it as one of those inevitable facts which politicians call *faits accomplis*. The words of an author previously cited will serve as proof of this.

Fine instrumental music must reckon with a much smaller number of competent listeners than opera; to enjoy it fully requires genuine artistic insight and a more active and experienced sensitivity. With the large audience, coloring will always pass as expression, for unless it consist of individuals capable of forming an abstract ideal—something not to be expected of a whole auditorium, no matter how select it may be—it will never listen to a symphony, quartet, or other composition of this order without outlining a program for itself during the performance, according to the grandiose, lively, impetuous, serenely soothing, or melancholy character of the music. By means of this trick, listeners identify most concerts of instrumental music with the expression of certain passionate feelings; they imagine an action differing from those imagined by others as individuals differ among themselves. I speak here of the most cultivated, since for many, frequently for the majority, instrumental music is only a sensual pleasure, if not indeed a tiresome enigma. For them, instrumental music has neither coloring nor expression, and I simply do not know what they look for in it.[g]

Is it not evident from this that it is merely a question of officially recognizing an already existing power with a view to allowing it greater freedom of action and assisting it in the removal of its liabilities, so that henceforward it may work toward its future, toward its fame, not secretly, but in the deliberate repose that comes with an established success?

. . . . .

Through song there have always been *combinations* of music with literary or quasi-literary works; the present time seeks a *union* of the two which promises to become a more intimate one than any that have offered themselves thus far. Music in its masterpieces tends more and more to appropriate the masterpieces of literature. What harm can come to music, at the height to which it has grown since the beginning of the modern era, if it attach itself to a species that has sprung precisely from an undeniably modern way of feeling? Why should music, once so inseparably bound to the tragedy of Sophocles and the ode of Pindar, hesitate to unite itself in a different yet more adequate way with works born of an inspiration unknown to antiquity, to identify itself with such names as Dante

---

g Fétis.

and Shakespeare? Rich shafts of ore lie here awaiting the bold miner, but they are guarded by mountain spirits who breathe fire and smoke into the faces of those who approach their entrance and, like Slander, whom Voltaire compares to coals, blacken what they do not burn, threatening those lusting after the treasure with blindness, suffocation, and utter destruction.

To our regret we must admit that a secretly smoldering but irreconcilable quarrel has broken out between *vocational* and *professional* musicians. The latter, like the Pharisees of the Old Law, cling to the letter of the commandment, even at the risk of killing its spirit. They have no understanding of the love revealed in the New Testament, for the thirst after the eternal, the dream of the ideal, the search for the poetically beautiful in every form. They live only in fear, grasp only fear, preach only fear; for them, fear (not precisely the fear of the Lord, however) is the beginning and end of all wisdom; they hang on the language of the law with the pettiness of those whose hearts have not taught them that the fulfillment of the prophecy lies in the abolition of the sacrifice, in the rending of the veil of the temple; their wisdom consists in dogmatic disputes, in sterile and idle speculation on subtleties of the rules. They deny that one may show greater honor to the old masters by seeking out the germs of artistic development which they embedded in their works than by servilely and thoughtlessly tracing the empty forms whose entire content of air and light they drained themselves in their own day. On the other hand the *vocational* musicians hold that to honor these patriarchs one must regard the forms they used as exhausted and look on imitations of them as mere copies of slight value. They do not hope to glean further harvests from fields sown by giants and believe that they cannot continue the work already begun unless, as the patriarchs did in their time, they create new forms for new ideas, put new wine into new bottles.

To Berlioz and his successes has been opposed from the beginning, like an insurmountable dam, that academic aversion to every art product which, instead of following the beaten path, is formed in accordance with an unaccustomed ideal or called up by incantations foreign to the old rite. But with or without the magisterial permission of the titulary and nontitulary professors—even without that of the illustrious director of the Paris Conservatoire, who visited Berlioz' concerts quite regularly in order, as he put it, "to learn how not to do it"—everyone who would keep up with contemporary art must study the scores of this master, precisely to see what is being done today and "to learn how to do it." And in truth, the so-called classicists themselves are not above making use of overheard and stolen ideas and effects and even, in exceptional cases, of conceding that Berlioz does after all show talent for instrumentation and skill in combining, since he is one of those artists, previously mentioned, who through the wider expression of their feelings and the freer unfolding of their individuality expand and enrich the form and make it serviceable. In the last analysis, however, the hypocrisy of his envious opponents consists in refusing to pay him the tuition they owe and have on their conscience while they publicly tread into the mire everything of his which they are not and never will be capable of imitating and privately pull out all feathers of his which they can use as ornaments themselves. We could name many who rise up against Berlioz, though their best works would be disfigured were one to take from them everything for which they are obliged to him. We repeat, therefore, that unusual treatment of form is not the supreme unpardonable error of which Berlioz is accused; his opponents will indeed concede, perhaps, that he has done art a service in discovering new inflections. What they will never forgive is that form has for him an importance subordinate to idea, that he does not, as they do, cultivate form for form's sake; they will never forgive him for being a thinker and a poet.

Strangely enough, that *union* of music and literature of which we have already spoken, constantly increasing in intimacy, developing itself with surprising rapidity, is gaining firm footing despite the equally lively opposition of *professional* musicians and men of letters. Both parties set themselves against it with the same vigor, with the same obstinacy. The latter, looking askance, see their property being taken over into a sphere where, apart from the value *they* placed on it, it acquires new significance; the former are horrified at a violation of their territory by elements with which they do not know how to deal. The tone-poets have hence to contend with a double enmity; they find themselves between two fires. But the strength of their cause compensates for the weakness of their position. Whether one recognizes it or not, the fact remains that both arts, more than ever before, feel themselves mutually attracted and are striving for inner union.

Through the endless variety of its forms, art reproduces the endless variety of constitutions and impressions. There are characters and feelings which can attain full development only in the dramatic; there are others which in no wise tolerate the limitations and restrictions of the stage. Berlioz recognized this. From the church, where it was for so many centuries exclusively domiciled and from whence its masterpieces scarcely reached the outer world, musical art moved by degrees into the theater, setting up there a sort of general headquarters or open house where anyone might exhibit his inspirations in any genre he chose. For a while it would scarcely have entered the head of any musician to regard himself as incapable of composing dramatic works. It seemed as though, on admission to the musical guild or brotherhood, one also acquired and accepted the ability, sanction, and duty to supply a certain number of operas, large or small, romantic or comic, *serie* or *buffe*. All hastened to the contest in this arena, hospitably open to everyone. When the terrain of the boards proved slippery, later on, some crept and others danced on the tightrope; many provided themselves with hammers instead of balancing poles and, when their neighbors struggled to keep their balance, hit them over the head. Some bound golden skates to their feet and with their aid left way behind them a train of poor devils, panting to no avail; certain ones, like messengers of the gods, had at their head and heels the wings given them at birth by genius, by means of which, if they did not precisely make rapid progress, they were able at least to fly on occasion to the summit. And, for all that these last remained, here as elsewhere, very much in the minority, they none the less imposed on their successors so great an obligation to surpass their accomplishment that a moment seems to have arrived which should cause many to ask themselves whether the sense of duty which urges them to join in this turmoil is not a prepossession. Those, indeed, who expect more of fame than a draft to be discounted by the present, more than a gilt-paper crown to be snatched at by fabricators of artificial flowers—let them ask themselves whether they were really born to expend their energies in this field, to course and tourney in these narrow lists; whether their temperament does not impel them toward more ideal regions; whether their abilities might not take a higher flight in a realm governed by fewer constraining laws; whether their freer fantasy might not then discover one of those Atlantides, blissful isles, or unknown constellations for which all students of the earth and sky are seeking. We for our part are persuaded that not every genius can limit his flight within the narrow confines of the stage and that he who cannot is thus forced to form for himself a new *habitaculum*.

To seek to import a foreign element into instrumental music and to domesticate it there by encroaching upon the independence of feeling through definite subjects offered to the intelligence in advance, by forcing upon a composer a concept to be literally represented or poetically formulated, by directing the attention of the listener, not only to the woven pattern of the music, but also to the ideas communicated by its contours and successions—this seems to many an absurd, if not a sacrilegious undertaking. Small wonder that before Berlioz they cover their heads and let their beards grow—before him who carries this beginning so far that, by symbolizing its presence, he causes the human voice to be heard in the hitherto wholly impersonal symphony; before him who undertakes to impart to the symphony a new interest, to enliven it with an entirely new element; before him who—not content to pour out in the symphony the lament of a common woe, to cause to sound forth in it the hopes of all and to stream forth from its focus the affections and shocks, sorrows and ardors, which pulse in the heart of mankind—takes possession of its powers in order to employ them in the expression of the sufferings and emotions of a specific, exceptional individual! Since the pleasure of listening to orchestral works has always been an altogether subjective one for those who followed the poetic content along with the musical, it seems to many a distortion, a violence done to its character, that the imagination is to be forced to adapt completely outlined pictures to that which is heard, to behold and accept figures in precisely the way the author wills. The hitherto usual effect of pure instrumental music on poetic temperaments may perhaps be compared to that which antique sculpture produces in them; in their eyes, these works also represent passions and forms, generating certain movements of the affections, rather than the specific and particular individuals whose names they bear—names, moreover, which are for the most part again allegorical representations of ideas. For them, Niobe is not this or that woman stricken by this or that misfortune; she is the most exalted expression of supreme suffering. In Polyhymnia they see, not a specific person engaged in specific speech or action, but the visible representation of the beauty, harmony, charm, and magic of that compelling, yet soft and placid persuasion whose eloquence can be concentrated in a single glance. Minerva, for them, is not only the divine, blue-eyed mentor of Ulysses, she is also the noblest symbol of that gift of our spirit which simultaneously judges and divines; who, provided with all the attributes of force, armed with all the weapons of war, is still a friend of peace; who, bearing lance and breastplate, causes her most beautiful gift, the olive tree, to sprout, promising peace; who, possessor of the terrifying aegis, loses nothing of the kindliness and attraction of her smile, of the slowly sinking cadence of her movements.

· · · · ·

Just as marble presents artistic formulations of general concepts to the eye, so the ear, in instrumental music, desires something similar. For the cultivated listener, one symphony expresses to a supreme degree the several phases of passionate, joyous feeling, another—elegiac mourning, another—heroic enthusiasm, still another—sorrow over an irreparable loss. If, then, these cultivated listeners are accustomed to seek and find in an art work the abstract expression of universal human feeling, they must experience a natural distaste for everything that aims to lend this universality concrete character, to make it particular, to derive it from a specific human figure. They have admittedly the undeniable right, the inalienable duty, to wish to see this species of creative activity maintained; shall other species for this reason be scolded out of their right to existence? Shall those who feel driven by their genius and by the spirit of the age to discover new molds be bowed beneath the yoke of a uniform way of working? Or should one not rather fear to see them renounce ambitions which they would admirably succeed in realizing in order to deny their birthright in efforts not in agreement with the nature of their inspiration?

.   .   .   .

10. Richard Wagner

The Art Work of the Future belongs to the most critical period in Wagner's life, the first years of his exile and of his residence in Zurich, the years between the end of his work on *Lohengrin* (1847) and the beginning of his work on the *Ring* (1853). During this lull in his artistic productivity, Wagner endeavored to come to terms with the problem of the opera and with himself; the results of this soul-searching are his three capital essays—*Art and Revolution* (1849), *The Art Work of the Future* (1850), and *Opera and Drama* (1852)—and in a larger sense, the great music-dramas of his maturity and old age. Three times, later on, he attempted to summarize the contents of these essays—first in *A Communication to My Friends* (1852), then in *"Music of the Future"* (1860), finally in *On the Destiny of Opera* (1869); in 1879, near the end of his life, he returned to the problem once more in a series of three further essays—*On the Writing of Poetry and Music, On the Writing of Operatic Poetry and Music in Particular*, and *On the Application of Music to the Drama*.

It is well known that the three major essays of Wagner's earlier years in Zurich were written under the immediate influence of the philosopher Ludwig Feuerbach (1804–1872), author of *The Essence of Christianity* (1841), whose repeated attacks upon orthodox theology had attracted the interest of Marx and Engels and had made him, somewhat to his astonishment, the idol of the "Young German" intellectuals sympathetic to the uprisings of 1849. In his autobiography, Wagner tells us himself that his acquaintance with Feuerbach's reputation dates from his last years in Dresden; traces of Feuerbach's influence have even been detected in Wagner's *Jesus of Nazareth*, a dramatic synopsis sketched at just this time. As to *The Art Work of the Future*, this owes its very title to Feuerbach's *Principles of the Philosophy of the Future* (1843), and in its original edition as a separate monograph it was introduced by a letter from Wagner to Feuerbach, beginning: "To no one but you, my dear sir, can I dedicate this work, for with it I give you back your own property."

In later life, after his conversion to Schopenhauer and to a more prudent political philosophy, Wagner did what he could to play down the revolutionary character of his earlier writings and to represent his youthful enthusiasm for Feuerbach as an unimportant passing phase. This is already evident to some extent in the summary incorporated in his *"Music of the Future."* It became still more evident with the publication of the third and fourth volumes of his *Sämmtliche Schriften* in 1872; here the dedication to Feuerbach is silently suppressed, while the foreword to the third volume contains this apologia: "From my reading of several of the works of Ludwig Feuerbach, which held a lively interest for me at the time, I had taken over various designations for concepts which I then applied to artistic ideas to which they could not always clearly correspond. Herein I surrendered myself without critical reflection to a brilliant author who appealed to my mood of the moment, particularly in that he bade farewell to philosophy (in which he believed himself to have discovered nothing but disguised theology) and addressed himself instead to a view of human nature in which I was persuaded that I could recognize again the artistic man I had had in mind. Thus there arose a certain reckless confusion, which revealed itself in a hastiness and lack of clarity in the use of philosophical schemes." Wagner then goes on to criticize his earlier use of Feuerbach's terminology, particularly of the expressions "willfulness" (*Willkür*) and "instinct" (*Unwillkür*), for which he now suggests the substitution, by the reader, of Schopenhauer's "will" (*Wille*) and "conscious will" (*Verstandeswille*). Still more exaggerated is Wagner's account of his relation to Feuerbach in his posthumously published autobiography: "Before long," he says, "it had already become impossible for me to return to his writings, and I recall that his book *On the Essence of Religion*, which appeared soon after this, so repelled me by the monotony of its title that when Herwegh opened it for me I clapped it shut before his eyes." How far from the truth this is, can be gathered from Wagner's letter of June 8, 1853, addressed to the imprisoned Röckel, his fellow revolutionary, and accompanied by a copy of the book in question: "Feuerbach's book is to a certain extent a résumé of all that he has hitherto done in the field of philosophy. It is not one of his really celebrated works, such as *The Essence of Christianity* or *Thoughts upon Death and Immortality*, but it is a short cut to a complete knowledge of his mental development and of the latest results of his speculations. I should be glad to think of you as strengthened and encouraged by contact with this clear, vigorous mind."

In *A Communication to My Friends*, speaking of the contradictions between his new theories and his earlier scores, Wagner has this to say: "The contradictions to which I refer will not even exist for the man who has accustomed himself to look at phenomena from the point of view of their development in time. The man who, in judging a phenomenon, takes this developmental factor into consideration will meet with contradictions only when the phenomenon in question is an unnatural, unreasonable one, set apart from space and time; to disregard the developmental factor altogether, to combine its various and clearly distinguishable phases, belonging to different times, into one indistinguishable mass, this is in itself an unnatural, unreasonable way of looking at things, one that can be adopted by our monumental-historical criticism, but not by the healthy criticism of a sympathetic and sensitive heart. . . . Critics who make a pretence of judging my artistic activity as a whole have sometimes proceeded in this uncritical, inattentive, and insensitive way; taking as relevant to their judgment views on the nature of art which I had made known from a standpoint arrived at only after a gradual and deliberate development, they have applied these views to the very art-works in which the natural developmental process that led me to the standpoint in question began. . . . It does not occur to them at all, when they compare the newly acquired standpoint with the older one left behind, that these are in fact two essentially different points of view, each one of them logically developed in itself, and that it would have been much better to have explained the new standpoint in the light of the old one than it was to judge the one abandoned in the light of the one adopted."

Wagner's objection is well taken. Yet later on, as we have seen, he was himself guilty of an uncritical procedure very similar to the one complained of here. Wagner too endeavored to combine two clearly distinguishable phases of his development, the middle and the late, into one indistinguishable mass. But whereas his critics had sought, as he puts it, "to kill two flies at one blow," Wagner seeks to prove the essential identity of two points of view that are essentially opposed.

Nietzsche, in his *Genealogy of Morals* (1887), sums up Wagner's dilemma with telling irony: "Think of the enthusiasm with which Wagner formerly followed in the footsteps of the philosopher Feuerbach: Feuerbach's expression 'healthy sensuality'—to Wagner, as to many Germans ('Young Germans,' they called themselves), this sounded in the thirties and forties like the word of redemption. Did he finally *learn* a different view? For it seems at least that at the end he wished to *teach* a different one."

From Das Kunstwerk der Zukunft [1]

[*1850*]

MAN AND ART IN GENERAL

Nature, Man, and Art

As MAN is to nature, so art is to man.

When nature had of itself developed to that state which encompassed

---

1 Text: *Sämtliche Schriften und Dichtungen*, 6th ed., Leipzig, 1912-14. Wagner divides the essay into five chapters; the present abridged translation includes I, 1 and 6; II, 1 and 4; IV, somewhat abbreviated.

the conditions for man's existence, then man arose of himself; once human life engenders of itself the conditions for the appearance of the art work, the art work comes into being of itself.

Nature begets and shapes aimlessly and instinctively, according to need, hence of necessity; this same necessity is the begetting and shaping force in human life; only what is aimless and instinctive arises from genuine need, and only in need lies the cause of life.

Natural necessity man recognizes only in the continuity of natural phenomena; until he grasps this continuity, he thinks nature willful.

From that moment in which man became sensible of his divergence from nature and thereby took the first step of all in his development as man, freeing himself from the unconsciousness of natural animal life to pass over into conscious life—when he thus placed himself in opposition to nature and when, as an immediate result of this, his sense of his dependence on nature led to the development in him of thought—from that moment, as the first assertion of consciousness, error began. But error is the father of knowledge, and the history of the begetting of knowledge from error is the history of the human race from the myth of primeval time to the present day.

Man erred from the time when he placed the cause of natural phenomena outside the state of nature itself, assumed for material phenomena an ideal origin, namely a willful origin of his own conceiving, and took the infinite continuity of nature's unconscious and purposeless activity for the purposeful behavior of will's noncontinuous, finite manifestations. Knowledge consists in the correction of this error, this correction in the perception of necessity in those phenomena for which we had assumed a willful origin.

Through this knowledge nature becomes conscious of self—to be precise, in man, who arrived at his knowledge of nature only through his distinction between self and nature, which he thus made an object. But this distinction disappears again at the moment when man recognizes nature's state as identical with his own; recognizes the same necessity in all that genuinely exists and lives, hence in human existence no less than in natural existence; and recognizes not only the connection of the natural phenomena with one another, but also his own connection with them.

If, through its connection with man, nature attains now to consciousness, and if the activity of this consciousness is to be human life itself—as though a representation, a picture, of nature—then human life itself attains to understanding through science, which makes of human life in turn an object of experience. But the activity of the consciousness won through science, the representation of the life made known through this activity, the copy of its necessity and truth is *art*.[a]

Man will not be that which he can and should be until his life is a faithful mirror of nature, a conscious pursuit of the only real necessity, *inner natural necessity*, not a subordination to an *outer* imagined *force*, imitating imagination, and hence not necessary but *willful*. Then man will really be man; thus far he has always merely existed by virtue of some predicate derived from religion, nationality, or state. In the same way, art too will not be that which it can and should be until it is or can be a faithful, manifestly conscious copy of genuine man and of the genuine, naturally necessary life of man, in other words, until it need no longer borrow from the errors, perversities, and unnatural distortions of our modern life the conditions of its being.

Genuine man, therefore, will not come into being until his life is shaped and ordered by true human nature and not by the willful law of state; genuine art will not live until its shapings need be subject only to the law of nature and not to the despotic caprice of fashion. For just as man becomes free only when he becomes joyously conscious of his connection with nature, so art becomes free only when it has no longer to be ashamed of its connection with life. Only in joyous consciousness of his connection with nature does man overcome his dependence on it; art overcomes its dependence on life only in its connection with the life of genuine, free men.

. . . . .

A Standard for the Art Work of the Future

It is not the individual mind, striving through art for fulfillment in nature, that has the power to create the art work of the future; only the collective mind, satisfied in life, has this power. But the individual can form an idea of it, and it is precisely the character of his striving—his striving for *nature*—which prevents this idea from being a mere fancy. He who longs to return to nature and who is hence unsatisfied in the modern present, finds not only in the totality of nature, but above all in *man's nature*, as it presents itself to him historically, those images which, when he beholds them, enable him to reconcile himself to life in general. In this nature he recognizes an image of all future things, already formed on a small scale; to imagine this scale expanded to its furthest compass lies within the conceptual limits of the impulse of his need for nature.

---

a Art in general, that is, or the art of the future in particular.

History plainly presents two principal currents in the development of mankind—the *racial-national* and the *unnational-universal*. If we now look forward to the completion of this second developmental process in the future, we have plainly before our eyes the completed course of the first one in the past. To what heights man has been able to develop, subjected to this first, almost directly formative influence—insofar as racial origin, linguistic affiliation, similarity of climate, and the natural character of a common native land permitted him to yield unconsciously to nature's influence—we have every reason to take the keenest pleasure in acknowledging. In the natural morality of all peoples, insofar as they include the normal human being—even those cried down as rawest—we learn for the first time to recognize the truth of human nature in its full nobility, its genuine beauty. Not *one* genuine virtue has been adopted by any religion whatever as a divine command which had not been included of itself in this natural morality; not *one* genuinely human concept of right has been developed by the later civilized state—and then, unfortunately, to the point of complete distortion!—which had not already been given positive expression in this natural morality; not *one* discovery genuinely useful to the community has been appropriated by later culture—with arrogant ingratitude!—which had not been derived from the operation of the native intelligence of the guardians of this natural morality.

That *art* is not an *artificial* product—that the need of art is not one willfully induced, but rather one native to the natural, genuine, unspoiled human being—who demonstrates this more strikingly than precisely these peoples? Indeed, from what circumstance could our mind deduce the demonstration of art's necessity, if not from the perception of this artistic impulse and its splendid fruits among these naturally developed peoples, among the people in general? Before what phenomenon do we stand with a more humiliating sense of the impotence of our frivolous culture than before the art of the *Hellenes?* To this, to this art of all-loving Mother Nature's favored children, those most beautiful human beings whose proud mother holds them up to us, even in these nebulous and hoary days of our present fashionable culture, as an undeniable and triumphant proof of what she can do—to the splendid art of the Greeks we look, to learn from intimate understanding of it how the art work of the future must be constituted! Mother Nature has done all she could—she has borne the Hellenes, nourished them at her breasts, formed them through her maternal wisdom; now she sets them before us with maternal pride and out of maternal love calls to us all: "This I have done for you; now, out of love for yourselves, do what you can!"

Thus it is our task to make of *Hellenic* art the altogether *human* art; to remove from it the conditions under which it was precisely a *Hellenic*, and not an altogether *human* art; to widen the *garb of religion,* in which alone it was a communal Hellenic art, and after removing which, as an egoistic individual art species, it could no longer fill the need of the community, but only that of luxury—however beautiful!—to widen this garb of the specifically *Hellenic religion* to the bond of the religion of the future—that of *universality*—in order to form for ourselves even now a just conception of the art work of the future. Yet, unfortunate as we are, it is precisely the power to close this bond, this *religion of the future,* that we lack, for after all, no matter how many of us may feel this urge to the art work of the future, we are *singular* and *individual*. An art work is religion brought to life; religions, however, are created, not by the artist, but by the *folk*.

Let us, then, be content that for the present—without egoistic vanity, without wishing to seek satisfaction in any selfish illusion whatsoever, but with sincere and affectionate resignation to the hope for the art work of the future—we test first of all the nature of the art varieties which today, in their dismembered condition, make up the present general state of art; that we brace ourselves for this test by a glance at the art of the Hellenes; and that we then boldly and confidently draw our conclusions as to the *great universal art work of the future!*

MAN AS ARTIST AND THE ART DIRECTLY DERIVED FROM HIM

Man as the Subject and Material of His Own Art

There is an *outer* and an *inner* man. The senses to which man presents himself as artistic subject are *sight* and *hearing;* to the eye he presents the outer man, to the ear the inner.

The eye apprehends *man's corporeal form*, compares it with its surroundings, and distinguishes it from them. The corporeal man and his instinctive manifestations, in physical pain and pleasure, of impressions received through external stimulation present themselves directly to the eye. Indirectly he communicates to it also, through facial expression and gesture, the sensations of the inner man, not directly perceptible to it; above all through the expression of the eye itself, which meets the beholding eye directly, he can communicate to the latter not only the feelings of his heart, but even the characteristic activity of his mind, and the more precisely the outer man can express the inner, the more clearly he reveals himself as artist.

Directly the inner man presents himself to the ear through the *tone of his voice. Tone* is the direct expression of feeling, as it has its physical seat in the heart, the starting and returning point for the circulation of the blood. Through the sense of hearing tone penetrates from heart to heart, from feeling to feeling; grief and joy communicate themselves directly, through the manifold tone of voice, from one man of feeling to another, and where the outer corporeal man's capacity for expression and communication finds its limit in the character of the inner feeling of the heart to be expressed and communicated to the eye, there steps in the decisive communication to the ear through the tone of voice, and through the ear to the feeling of the heart.

Moreover, where the direct expression of the tone of voice finds its limit in turn in the communication and exactly distinguishable definition, to the sympathetic and interested inner man, of the single feelings of the heart, there steps in, transmitted through the tone of voice, the expression of *speech. Speech* is the concentrated element of voice, word the consolidated *mass* of tone. In speech, feeling communicates through hearing to feeling, but to a feeling that is to be similarly concentrated and consolidated, to which it wishes to convey itself with a view to positive unmistakable understanding. It is accordingly the organ of the specific feeling which understands and would be understood—the understanding. For less definite, general feeling the direct character of tone sufficed; such feeling dwelt on tone, as the expression in itself already satisfying and pleasing to the senses; in the quantity of its expansion it had even the power to convey its own quality significantly. The specific need which seeks to make itself intelligible in speech is more decided, more imperious; it does not dwell comfortably on its sensual expression, for it must represent the feeling which is its subject and differentiate it from general feeling, hence portray and describe that which tone, as the expression of general feeling, conveyed directly. For this reason the speaker must derive his images from related, but at the same time differentiated objects and assemble them. For this complex mediating process he must, generally speaking, enlarge upon his subject; on the other hand, dominated by his principal aim—to promote understanding—he hastens the process by dwelling on tone as briefly as possible, by leaving its general capacity for expression wholly out of account. Through this necessary renunciation, through this giving up of his pleasure in the sensual element in his own expression—this giving up, at least, of that degree of pleasure which the man of body and the man of feeling were able to take in their manner of expression—the man of understanding becomes able, by virtue of his organ, to give to speech that positive expression in which the men of body and feeling progressively found their limits. The power of the man of understanding is unlimited; he collects and singles out the general; he divides and connects the images which his senses transmit to him from the outer world in accordance with his need and preference; he joins and looses the particular and the general as he sees fit, to satisfy his desire for a positive, intelligible expression of his feeling, his view, his will. Only there does he find his limit in turn, there in the agitation of his feeling, in the animation of joy or in the violence of grief—there where the particular and willful retire before the general and instinctive in the dominant feeling itself, where, leaving behind the egoism of his restricted personal sensation, he finds himself again in the communism of the great all-embracing sensation, hence of the unrestricted truth of feeling and of sensation in general—there where he must subordinate his individual arbitrary will to necessity, whether of grief or of joy, and has accordingly, not to command, but to obey—there where he desires the one appropriate direct expression of his infinitely intensified feeling. Here he must once again avail himself of general expression and must retrace his steps in order, passing through the same stages by means of which he arrived at his particular standpoint, borrowing from the man of feeling the sensual tone of feeling, from the man of body the sensual gesture of body; for where there is required the most direct and at the same time most positive expression of the highest and truest that man can possibly express, there must be indeed united the whole, complete man: the man of understanding, bound through the most intimate, all-pervading love to the men of feeling and body—no one of them for self alone.

The progress of the outer man of body through the man of feeling to the man of understanding is one of constantly increasing mediation; the man of understanding, like speech, his organ of expression, is the most mediate and dependent of all, for all the qualities subordinated to him must be normally developed before the conditions of *his* normal quality are present. But the most restricted capacity is at the same time the most intense, and his joy in self, which comes from recognition of his higher, pre-eminent quality, drives him to the arrogant presumption that he may employ the qualities basic to him as slaves of his arbitrary will. This arrogance, however, gives way before the omnipotence of physical sensation and the feeling of the heart the moment they manifest themselves to him as common to all mankind, as sensations and feelings of the species. The individual sensation and the individual feeling, as they reveal themselves in him as an individual through this one particular and personal contact with this one particular and personal object—these he has the power to suppress and to control in favor of a richer combination, which he conceives, of many-sided objects; the richest combination of all the objects perceptible to him finally sets before him *man as species and in his connection with nature as a whole,* and before this great all-powerful object his arrogance breaks down. Thenceforward he can will only the universal, the true, the absolute—his own absorption, not in the love of this or that object, but in love *in general;* thus the egoist becomes communist, the one —all, the man—god, and the art variety—art.

. . . . . .

The Art of Tone

The sea divides and connects the continents; thus the art of tone divides and connects the two extreme antitheses of human art, the arts of dancing and of poetry.

It is man's *heart;* the blood, circulating from this center, gives to the flesh, turned outward, its warm, lively color—at the same time it nourishes the brain nerves, tending inward, with waves of resilient energy. Without the activity of the heart, the activity of the brain would remain a mere mechanical performance, the activity of the body's external organs equally mechanical and unfeeling. Through the heart, the intellect is made sensible of its relation to the body as a whole—the mere man of the senses attains to intellectual activity.

But the organ of the heart is *tone,* and its artistically conscious speech is the *art of tone.* This is the full, flowing heart-love that ennobles sensual pleasure and humanizes spiritual thought. Through the art of tone, the arts of poetry and dancing understand each other; in the one there blend in affectionate fusion the laws governing the manifestations natural to the others—in the one the will of the others becomes instinctive will, the measure of poetry and the beat of dancing become the inevitable rhythm of the heartthrob.

If music receives from its sister arts the conditions of its manifestation, it gives these back to them, made infinitely beautiful, as the conditions of their manifestation; if dancing supplies music with its law of motion, music returns it in the form of rhythm, spiritually and sensually embodied as a measure for ennobled and intelligible movement; if poetry supplies music with its meaningful series of clear-cut words, intelligibly united through meaning and measure as material bodies, rich in idea, for the consolidation of its infinitely fluid tonal element, music returns this ordered series of quasi-intellectual, unfulfilled speech-sounds—indirectly representative, concentrated as image but not yet as immediate, inevitably true expression—in the form of *melody*, directly addressed to feeling, unerringly vindicated and fulfilled.

In musically animated *rhythm* and *melody*, dancing and poetry regain their own being, sensually objectified and made infinitely beautiful and capable; they recognize and love each other. But rhythm and melody are the *arms* with which Music encircles her sisters in affectionate entwinement; they are the *shores* by means of which she, the *sea*, unites two continents. Should the sea recede from the shores, should the abysmal waste spread out between it and them, no jaunty sailing ship will longer range from the one continent to the other; they will forever remain divided—unless mechanical inventions, perhaps railroads, succeed in making the waste passable; then, doubtless, one will also pass clean across the sea in steamships; the breath of the all-animating breeze will give place to the puff of the machine; what difference need it make that the wind naturally blows eastward?—the machine clatters westward, precisely where we wish to go; thus the ballet maker sends across the steam-conquered sea of music to the poetry continent for the program of his new pantomime, while the stage-piece fabricator fetches from the dancing continent as much leg seasoning as he happens to need to liven up a stale situation. Let us see what has happened to Sister Music since the death of all-loving Father *Drama!*

Not yet may we give up our figure of the *sea* as music's being. If *rhythm* and *melody* are the shores at which the tonal art meets with and makes fruitful the two continents of the arts primevally related to it, then tone itself is the primeval fluid element, and the immeasurable expanse of this fluid is the sea of *harmony*. Our eye is aware only of its surface; its depth only our heart's depth comprehends. Up from its bottom, dark as night, it spreads out to its mirroring surface, bright as the sun; from the one shore radiate on it the rings of rhythm, drawn wider and wider—from the shadowy valleys of the other shore rises the longing breeze which agitates the placid surface in waves of melody, gracefully rising and falling.

Into this sea man dives to yield himself again, radiant and refreshed, to the light of day; he feels his heart expand with wonder when he looks down into these depths, capable of unimaginable possibilities, whose bottom his eye is never to fathom, whose fathomlessness fills him accordingly with astonishment and forebodings of the infinite. This is the depth and infinity of nature itself, which veils from man's searching eye the impenetrable mystery of its budding, begetting, and longing, precisely because the eye can comprehend only what has become visible—the budded, the begotten, the longed for. This nature is in turn none other than the *nature of the human heart itself,* which encompasses the feelings of love and longing in their most infinite being, which is itself love and longing, and which—since in its insatiable longing it desires itself alone—grasps and comprehends itself alone.

If this sea rises of itself from its own depths, if it derives the cause of its motion from the primeval cause of its own element, this motion is also endless, implacable, eternally returning to itself unsatisfied, eternally longing and rousing itself anew. But should an object situated outside the monstrous abundance of this longing enkindle it; should this defining object draw near it from the positive, concrete, phenomenal world; should man himself, radiant with sunlight, moving sinuously and vigorously, enflame this longing with a glance of his burning eye and agitate with his swelling breath the elastic mass of the sea crystal; then—no matter how high the towering glow, no matter how powerfully uprooted the surface by the storm—once the fierce glow has subsided, the flame will burn at last as a mildly shining light; once the giant waves have broken in spray, the surface will be ruffled at last only by the innocent play of the ripples; and man, happy in the sweet harmony of his whole being, will surrender himself in a frail shell to the trusted elements and will steer secure, guided by that familiar, mildly shining light.

The *Hellene,* when he set sail on his sea, never lost sight of the coast; this was for him the safe current which bore him from strand to strand, on which, between the familiar shores, he rode along to the melodious measure of the helm, now watching the dance of the wood nymphs, now listening to the hymn of the gods, whose ingeniously melodious word-round the breezes bore to him from the temple on the mountain top. On the surface of the water there lay faithfully reflected before him, framed in a blue ethereal border, the shore country with its rocks, valleys, trees, flowers, and men, and he took this charmingly weaving reflection, attractively animated by the fresh fanning of the breezes, for *harmony.*

The *Christian* bade the shores of life farewell. He sought a wider and less restricted sea, to be at last absolutely alone on the ocean between sea and sky. The *word,* the word of *faith,* was his compass, directing him steadfastly toward heaven. This heaven floated above him; at each horizon it sank down to bound the sea; the sailor, however, never reached this boundary; from century to century he drifted unredeemed toward the new homeland always hovering before him but never reached, until, seized with doubt as to the virtue of his compass, he grimly threw this too overboard as man's last illusion and now, free of all ties, gave himself up, helmless, to the inexhaustible willfulness of the sea waves. In the unsatisfied, exasperated fury of his love he stirred up the depths of the sea against the unattainable sky; he incited the insatiability of its very desire for love and longing, which without an object must forever and ever love and long for itself alone—this deepest, least redeemable hell of the most restless egoism, which expands without end, wishes and wills, and forever and ever can wish and will itself alone—against the abstract blue heaven-generality, against the supremely object-needing general desire—against absolute inobjectivity itself. To wish to be blissful, absolutely blissful, *blissful* in the widest and most unlimited sense, and at the same time to remain wholly *itself*—this was the insatiable desire of the Christian temperament. Thus the sea rose up from its depths to the sky, thus it sank back, again and again, from the sky to its depths, eternally itself and hence eternally unsatisfied—like the boundless, all-sovereign longing of the heart, self-condemned to be forever unable to give itself or to be absorbed in an object, self-condemned to be *itself* alone.

But in nature everything immeasurable seeks its measure, everything limitless draws limits for itself, the elements concentrate themselves at last as definite phenomena; thus also the boundless sea of Christian longing found the new coastland against which it might break its impatience. There on the far horizon, where we had fondly imagined the entrance into the limitless heaven-space, always sought but never found, there at last the boldest of all navigators discovered land—inhabited by peoples—actual, blissful land. Through his discovery the wide ocean was not only measured, but also made for mankind an inland sea about which the coasts spread themselves out only in inconceivably wider circles. But if Columbus taught us to sail the ocean and thus to connect all the earth's continents; if through his discovery the short-sighted national man has, from the point of view of world history, become the all-seeing universal man—has become man altogether; so through the hero who sailed the wide shoreless sea of absolute music to its limits were won the new undreamed-of coasts which now no longer divide this sea from the old primevally human continents, but *connect* them for the newborn fortunate artistic humanity of the future. This hero is none other than—*Beethoven*.[2]

When Music freed herself from the round of her sisters—just as her frivolous sister, Dancing, had taken from her the rhythmic measure—she took with her from her brooding sister, Poetry, as an indispensable, immediate life condition, the *word;* not by any means, however, the man-

---

2 See *Oper und Drama*, I, 5 (or, as translated by Edwin Evans, I, 116–117, §§ 208–210), where   Wagner returns to this comparison of Beethoven to Columbus and develops it further.

creative, ideally poetic word, but only the materially indispensable word, the concentrated tone. If she had relinquished the rhythmic beat to her parting sister, Dancing, to use as she pleased, she now built herself up solely through the word, the word of Christian faith, that fluid, spineless, illusive thing which soon, gladly and unresistingly, placed itself altogether in her power. The more the word took refuge in the mere stammering of humility, the mere lisping of implicit, childlike love, the more inevitable was Music's recognition of her need to shape herself from the inexhaustible depths of her own fluid being. The struggle for such a shaping is the building up of *harmony*.

Harmony grows from the bottom up as a true column of related tonal materials, fitted together and arranged in strata laid one above another. The ceaseless changing of such columns, constantly rising up anew, each one adjoining another, constitutes the sole possibility of absolute harmonic movement on a horizontal plane. The perception of the need to care for the beauty of this movement on a horizontal plane is foreign to the nature of absolute harmony; harmony knows only the beauty of the changing play of the colors of its columns, not the charm of their orderly arrangement as perceived in time—for this is the work of rhythm. The inexhaustible many-sidedness of this changing play of colors is, on the other hand, the eternally productive source from whence harmony, in boundless self-satisfaction, derives the power to present itself unceasingly as new; the breath of life, moving and animating this restless change—which, in its turn, is willfully self-conditioning—is the nature of tone itself, the breath of the impenetrable, all-powerful longing of the heart. The realm of harmony, then, knows no beginning or end; is like the objectless and self-consuming fervor of the temperament which, ignorant of its source, remains itself alone; is desiring, longing, raging, languishing—*perishing,* that is, dying without having satisfied itself in an object—dying, in other words, without dying; and hence, again and again, returns to self.

As long as the word was in power, it ruled beginning and end; when it sank to the fathomless bottom of harmony, when it remained only a "groaning and sighing of the soul"—as at the fervent height of Catholic church music—then, at the topmost stratum of those harmonic columns, the stratum of unrhythmic melody, the word was willfully tossed as though from wave to wave, and harmony, with its infinite possibilities, had now to lay down for itself self-derived laws for its finite manifestation. The nature of harmony corresponds to no other capacity of man as artist; it sees itself reflected, neither in the physically determined movements of the body, nor in the logical progression of thought; it can conceive its just measure, neither, as thought does, in the recognized necessity of the world of material phenomena, nor, as bodily movement does, in the presentation, as perceived in time, of its instinctive, richly conditioned character; it is like a natural force, apprehended, but not comprehended, by man. From out its own fathomless depths, from an outer—not inner—necessity to limit itself for positive finite manifestation, harmony must shape for itself the laws it will obey. These laws of harmonic succession, based on relationship, just as the harmonic columns, or harmonies, were themselves formed from the relationship of tonal materials, combine now as a just measure, which sets a beneficial limit to the monstrous range of willful possibilities. They permit the widest possible selection from out the sphere of harmonic families, expand to the point of free choice the possibility of connections through elective relationship with members of distant families, demand above all, however, a strict conformity to the house rules of the family momentarily chosen and an implicit acceptance of them for the sake of a salutary end. To postulate or to define this end—in other words, the just measure of the expansion of the musical composition in time—lies beyond the power of the innumerable rules of harmonic decorum; these, as that part of music which can be scientifically taught or learned, while they can separate the fluid tonal mass of harmony, dividing it into bounded smaller masses, cannot determine the just measure of these bounded masses in time.

If music, grown to harmony, could not possibly go on to derive from itself its law of expansion in time, once the limiting power of speech had been swallowed up, it was obliged to turn to those remnants of the rhythmic beat that dancing had left behind for it; rhythmic figures had to enliven the harmony; their alternation, their return, their division and union had to affect the fluid expanse of harmony as the word had originally affected tone, concentrating it and bringing it to a definitely timed conclusion. This rhythmic enlivening, however, was not based on any inner necessity, crying out for purely human presentation; its motive power was not the man of feeling, thought, and will as he reveals himself in speech and bodily movement, but an *outer* necessity which harmony, demanding an egoistic conclusion, had made its own. This rhythmic alternation and shaping, not motivated by an inner necessity, could therefore be enlivened only according to willful laws and discoveries. These laws and discoveries are those of *counterpoint*.

Counterpoint, in its various progeny, normal and abnormal, is the artificial play of art with art, the mathematics of feeling, the mechanical rhythm of egoistic harmony. With its discovery abstract music was so pleased that it gave itself out as the one and only absolute and self-sufficient art—as the art owing its existence, not to any human need whatever, but simply to *itself*, to its divine and absolute nature. Quite naturally, the willful man considers himself the one man absolutely justified. Music, to be sure, owed to its arbitrary will alone only its seeming independence, for these tone-mechanical, contrapuntal pieces of art handiwork were altogether incapable of filling a *spiritual need*. In its pride, then, music had become its own direct antithesis; from a concern of the *heart* it had become a concern of the *mind*, from an expression of the boundless spiritual longing of the Christian it had become a balance sheet of the modern money market.

The living breath of the human voice, eternally beautiful and instinctively noble as it burst forth from the breast of the living folk, always young and fresh, blew this contrapuntal house of cards to the four winds. The *folk tune*, still true to self in undistorted grace—the *song* with positive limits, intimately entwined and one with poetry—lifted itself up on its elastic pinions into the regions of the scientifically musical world, with its need for beauty, and announced a joyous redemption. This world wished once more to set forth *men*, to cause men—not reeds—to sing; to this end it took possession of the folk tune and constructed from it the *operatic aria*. Just as the art of dancing had taken possession of the folk dance, to refresh itself, as it required, at this source and to employ it, as fashion dictated, in artistic combination, so also the elegant art of opera dealt with the folk tune; it now grasped, not the *whole* man, to indulge him artistically to the full according to his natural need, but only the *singing* man—and in the tune he sang, not the folk poem with its innate creative power, but only the melodious tune, abstracted from the poem, to which it now adapted as it pleased fashionably conventional, intentionally meaningless literary phrases; it was not the throbbing heart of the nightingale, but only its throbbing throat, that it understood and sought to imitate. Just as the art dancer trained his legs in the most varied and yet most uniform bends, twists, and whirls to vary the folk dance, which he could not of himself develop further, so the art singer trained his throat in endless ornaments and scrollwork of all sorts to paraphrase and change the tune taken from the lips of the folk, which he could from its nature never create anew; thus the place which contrapuntal cleverness had vacated was taken only by a mechanical dexterity of another kind. Here we need not characterize at greater length the repulsive, indescribably disgusting perversion and distortion of the folk tune as manifested in the modern operatic aria—for it is in point of fact only a mutilated folk tune, not by any means an original invention—as, in derision of all nature, of all human feeling, it frees itself from any linguistically poetic basis and, as a lifeless, soulless toy of fashion, tickles the ear of the idiotic world of the opera house; we need only admit with sorrowful sincerity that our modern public actually takes it for the whole of music.

But remote from this public and the makers and sellers of fashionable wares who serve it, the innermost being of music was to soar up from its bottomless depths, with all the undiminished abundance of its untried capacity, to a redemption in the radiance of the universal, *single* art of the future, and was to take this flight from that bottom which is the bottom of all purely human art—that of *plastic bodily movement*, represented in musical *rhythm*.

If, in the lisping of the stereotyped Christian word, eternally and eternally repeated to the point of utter thoughtlessness, the *human voice* had at length completely taken refuge in a merely sensual and fluid tone device by means of which alone the art of music, wholly withdrawn from poetry, continued to present itself, the tone devices, mechanically transmitted at its side as voluptuous accompaniments of the art of dancing, had developed an increasingly heightened capacity for expression. To these devices, the bearers of the dance tune, *rhythmic melody* had been assigned as an exclusive possession, and since, in their combined effect, these readily absorbed the element of Christian harmony, all responsibility for music's further development *from within itself* devolved on them. The *harmonized dance* is the basis of the richest art work of the modern *symphony*. This dance made in its turn an appetizing morsel for the counterpoint machine, which freed it from its obedient devotion to its mistress, the corporeal art of dancing, and caused it now to leap and turn at *its* command. Yet the warm life breath of the natural folk tune had only to inspire the leather harness of this dance, trained up in counterpoint, and it became at once the living flesh of the humanly beautiful art work. This art work, in its highest perfection, is the *symphony of Haydn, Mozart, and Beethoven*.

In the symphony of *Haydn*, the rhythmic dance melody moves with all the fresh serenity of youth; its interweavings, dissolvings, and recombinings, though carried out with the utmost contrapuntal skill, reveal themselves scarcely any longer as products of a thus skillful process, but rather as proper to the character of a dance governed by highly imaginative rules, so warmly are they permeated by the breath of genuinely and joyously human life. The middle movement of the symphony, in a more moderate tempo, we see assigned by Haydn to the swelling breadth of the simply melodious folk tune; following the rules of melos peculiar to singing, he expands this, intensifying it in higher flights and enlivening it in repetitions many-sided in their expression. The melody thus conditioned was elemental to the symphony of *Mozart*, with his wealth of song and delight in singing. He inspired his instruments with the ardent breath of the *human voice*, to which his genius was overwhelmingly inclined. The rich, indomitable tide of harmony he brought to bear on melody's heart, as though restlessly anxious to give synthetically to the purely instrumental melody that depth of feeling and fervor which, in the innermost heart, makes of the natural human voice an inexhaustible source of expression. As to all those things in his symphonies which lay more or less remote from the satisfying of this, his primary aim, if Mozart to a certain extent merely dispatched them with uncommonly skillful contrapuntal treatment according to the traditional usage, becoming stable even in him, he intensified the capacity of the purely instrumental for singing expression to such a point that it could encompass, not only serenity and placid easy intimacy, as had been the case with Haydn, but also the whole depth of the heart's infinite longing.

The immeasurable capacity of instrumental music for the expression of impulses and desires of elemental intensity was opened up by *Beethoven*. He it was who released to unrestricted freedom the innermost being of Christian harmony, that fathomless sea so boundlessly vast, so restlessly mobile. Borne by instruments alone, the *harmonic melody*—for thus we must call the melody isolated from the spoken line, to distinguish it from the rhythmic dance melody—was capable of the most unlimited expression and of the widest possible treatment. In long connected sequences and in larger, smaller, indeed smallest fragments, it became, under the poetic hands of the master, the sounds, syllables, words, and phrases of a language which could express the unheard, the unsaid, the unuttered. Each letter of this language was an endlessly spiritual element, and the measure of their fusion was a measuring as free and unrestricted as a composer desiring the most immeasurable expression of the most impenetrable longing could possibly exercise. Rejoicing in the unspeakably expressive possibilities of this language, yet suffering under the burden of his artist-soul's desire, which, in its boundlessness, could have no object but itself and might not seek to satisfy itself outside it—the overly happy yet unhappy sailor, loving the sea yet weary of it, sought a sure anchorage from the rapturous storms of fierce impatience. If the possibilities of the language were endless, so also was the longing that inspired it; then how proclaim the end—the satisfaction—of this longing in the same language which was no more than its expression? If in this absolute and quasi-elemental language we call up the expression of immeasurable heart's longing, then, like the endlessness of longing itself, the *endlessness* of this expression is its only necessary end; a finite *end*, as a stilling of longing, could be only willful. With the definite expression borrowed from the rhythmic dance melody, instrumental music can represent and end a mood in itself at rest and precisely limited, for it takes its just measure from bodily movement, an object lying originally outside itself. If from the first a piece of music surrenders wholly to this expression—which more or less inevitably must be understood as an expression of serenity—then, even when all the possibilities of tonal language are richly and luxuriously developed, satisfaction of every sort will be rooted necessarily in this expression; if in the end, however, this precisely limited expression even so much as approaches the storms of endless longing, this satisfaction can be only purely willful and hence actually unsatisfying. The transition from a mood of endless agitation and longing to one of joyous satisfaction cannot take place necessarily, except through absorption of the longing in an *object*. This object, in keeping with the character of endless longing, can only be one presenting itself as finite, concrete, and moral. In such an object, absolute music finds none the less its definitely determined limits; unless it adopts the most willful measures, it cannot now or ever bring of itself alone the concretely and morally determined man to exactly perceptible and clearly distinguishable presentation; in its endless intensification, it is still only *feeling* after all; it makes its appearance in the *train* of the moral deed, not as *the deed itself;* it can set moods and feelings side by side, but cannot in a necessary way develop one mood from another; it lacks *moral will*.

What inimitable art Beethoven employed in his C minor Symphony to guide his ship out of the ocean of endless longing into the harbor of fulfillment! He succeeded in intensifying the expression of his music almost to the point of moral resolve, yet was unable to proclaim this resolve itself. Without moral support, after each exertion of will, we are alarmed at the prospect that we may quite as well be headed, not for victory, but for relapse into suffering; indeed, such a relapse must seem to us rather more necessary than the morally unmotivated triumph, which—not a necessary achievement, but a willful gift of grace—can hence not lift us up or satisfy us *morally*, after the longing of the heart, as we require.

Who was less satisfied by this victory than Beethoven himself, may we presume? Was he tempted to another of this kind? The thoughtless army of his imitators, no doubt, who, having survived the tribulation of minor, concoct continual triumphs for themselves out of the glorious jubilation of major—but not the chosen master who was in his works to write the *world history of music.*

With reverent awe he refrained from plunging himself again into that sea of boundless and insatiable longing, bending his steps rather toward those lighthearted, vigorous beings whom he saw jesting, dancing, and making love in the green meadows at the edge of the fragrant woods, spread out under sunny skies. There, in the shadow of the trees, to the rustling of the foliage and the familiar rippling of the brook, he made a salutary covenant with nature; there he felt himself a man, his longing driven back deep into his breast before the power of the sweet inspiring *prospect.* In gratitude to this prospect, in faith and all humility, he named the single movements of the composition thus inspired for the scenes from life whose aspect had summoned them forth; the whole he called *Recollections of Country Life.*

And yet they were in truth no more than recollections—images, not immediate and concrete reality. Toward this reality, however, he was impelled with all the force of necessary artist's longing. To give his tonal forms that concentration, that immediately perceptible, sure, and concrete solidity, which, to his joy and comfort, he had observed in natural phenomena—this was the generous spirit of that joyous urge that created for us the incomparably magnificent A major Symphony. All violence, all longing and storming of the heart, have turned here to the rapturous exuberance of joy which carries us along in bacchanalian insistence through all the realms of nature, through all the streams and seas of life, self-confidently exultant everywhere we tread to the bold measure of this human dance of the spheres. This symphony is the very *apotheosis of the dance;* it is the highest being of the dance, the most blissful act of bodily movement, ideally embodied, as it were, in tone. Melody and harmony fill out together the bony frame of rhythm with firm human figures, slender and voluptuous, which almost before our eyes, here with supple giant limbs, there with delicate elastic flexibility, join the round to which the immortal melody sounds on and on, now charming, now bold, now serious,[b] now boisterous, now thoughtful, now exultant, until, in the last whirling of desire, a jubilant kiss brings to an end the last embrace.

---

[b] To the rhythm of the second movement, solemnly striding along, a secondary theme lifts up its longing plaint; about that rhythm, whose steady step is heard unceasingly throughout the whole, this yearning melody entwines itself, as does about the oak the ivy, which, but for its encircling of the powerful trunk, would curl and wind chaotically along the ground, luxuriantly forlorn, but which now, as a rich ornament of the rough oak's bark, gains sure and substantial form from the solidity of the tree itself. With what want of discernment this deeply significant discovery of Beethoven's has been exploited by our modern composers of instrumental music, with their eternal "secondary theme-making."

And yet these blissful dancers were but tonally represented, tonally imitated beings! Like another Prometheus, forming men from *clay* (*Thon*), Beethoven had sought to form men from *tone* (*Ton*). Neither from clay nor tone, however, but from both substances at once must man, the likeness of life-giving Zeus, be created. If the creatures of Prometheus were present to the *eye* alone, Beethoven's were so only to the *ear*. *But only there where eye and ear mutually assure each other of his presence do we have the whole artistic man.*

Where indeed should Beethoven have found those beings to whom he might have offered his hand across the element of his music? Those beings with hearts so open that he might have let the all-powerful stream of his harmonious tones flood into them? With forms so vigorously beautiful that his melodious rhythms might have *borne* them, not *tread* them under foot? Alas, no brotherly Prometheus, who might have shown such beings to him, came to his help from any side! He had himself to begin by discovering the *land of the man of the future*.

From the shores of dancing he plunged again into that endless sea from out whose depths he had once saved himself on these same shores, into the sea of insatiable heart's longing. But on this stormy voyage he set out aboard a strong-built ship, firmly joined as though by giant hands; with a sure grasp he bent the powerful tiller; he *knew* his journey's goal and was resolved to reach it. What he sought was not the preparation of imaginary triumphs for himself, not to sail back idly into the home port after boldly surmounted hardships; he sought to bound the limits of the ocean, to find the land which needs must lie beyond the watery wastes.

Thus the master forced his way through the most unheard-of possibilities of absolute tonal language—not by hurriedly stealing past them, but by proclaiming them completely, to their last sound, from his heart's fullest depths—until he reached that point at which the navigator begins to sound the sea's depths with his lead; at which he touches solid bottom at ever increasing heights as the strands of the new continent reach toward him from afar; at which he must decide whether to turn about into the fathomless ocean or whether to drop anchor in the new banks. But it was no rude hankering for the sea that had urged the master on to this long voyage; he wished and had to land in the new world, for it was to this end that the voyage had been undertaken. Resolutely he threw out his anchor, and this anchor was the *word*. This word, however, was not that willful, meaningless word which the fashionable singer chews over and over as the mere gristle of the vocal tone; it was the necessary, all-powerful, all-uniting word in which the whole stream of full heartfelt emotion is poured out; the safe harbor for the restless wanderer; the light lighting the night of endless longing; the word redeemed humanity proclaims from out the fullness of the world's heart; the word which Beethoven set as a crown upon the summit of his creations in tone. This word was— *"Joy!"* And with this word he called to all mankind: *"Be embraced, ye countless millions! And to all the world this kiss!"* And *this* word will become the language of the *art work of the future.*

This *last symphony* of Beethoven's is the redemption of music out of its own element as a *universal art.* It is the *human* gospel of the art of the future. Beyond it there can be no *progress,* for there can follow on it immediately only the completed art work of the future, *the universal drama,* to which Beethoven has forged for us the artistic key.

Thus from within itself music accomplished what no one of the other arts was capable of in isolation. Each of these arts, in its barren independence, helped itself only by taking and egoistic borrowing; not one was capable of being *itself* and of weaving from within itself the all-uniting bond. The art of tone, by being wholly *itself* and by moving from within its own primeval element, attained strength for the most tremendous and most generous of all self-sacrifices—that of self-control, indeed of self-denial—thus to offer to its sister arts a redeeming hand. Music has proved itself the *heart,* connecting head and limbs, and, what is not without significance, it is precisely music which, in the modern present, has spread to so unusual an extent through every branch of public life.

To form a clear conception of the *thoroughly inconsistent* spirit of this public life, we must consider, first of all, *that it was by no means a collective effort of the artists, as a body, and the public—indeed not even a collective effort of the musical artists themselves*—which brought to completion that tremendous process which we have just seen take place; *quite the other way, it was purely a superabundant artist individual* who individually absorbed the spirit of that collectivity wanting in the public, who actually began, indeed, by producing this collectivity in himself, out of the abundance of his own being, joined to the abundance of musical possibility, as something he himself longed for as an artist. We see that this wondrous creative process, as it is present in the symphonies of Beethoven as an increasingly determining, living force, was not only achieved by the master in the most complete isolation, but actually was not *understood* at all—or rather, was *misunderstood* in the most shameful way—by the company of artists. The forms in which the master proclaimed his artistic, world-historical struggle remained for the composers of his and the succeeding age mere *formulas,* passing through mannerism into fashion, and although no composer of instrumental music was so much as able to reveal the slightest originality, even in these forms, there was not one who lacked the courage to keep on writing symphonies and similar pieces, not one who even suspected that the *last* symphony had already been *written.*[c] Thus too, we have had to stand by while Beethoven's great voyage of world discovery—that unique, altogether inimitable feat which we saw accomplished in his "Symphony of Joy" as the final and boldest venture of his genius—was after the event reundertaken, with the most idiotic naïveté, and, without hardship, successfully weathered. A new genre, a "symphony with choruses"—this was all one saw in it. Why should not this or that composer also write his Symphony with Choruses? Why should not "God the Lord" be resoundingly praised at the end, after He has helped to conduct the three preliminary instrumental movements to the most facile of possible conclusions? [3] Thus Columbus discovered America only for the fulsome petty profiteering of our time.

The cause of this revolting *phenomenon* is deeply rooted in the very nature of our modern music. Detached from the arts of poetry and of dancing, the art of tone is no longer an art instinctively necessary to mankind. It has had to construct itself, following rules which, derived from its own peculiar nature, find their related and clarifying just measure in no purely human phenomenon. Each of the other arts held firm to the just measure of man's outward form, of man's outward life, or of nature itself, however willfully it might distort this unconditionally existing and accepted measure. The art of tone, which found its outward human measure in the timid ear alone, subject to fancies and deceptions of all sorts, had to form more abstract laws, combining these into a complete and scientific system. This system was the basis of modern music; on it one built, on it one piled tower upon tower, the bolder the construction, the more indispensable the foundation—a foundation in itself by no means that of nature. The sculptor, the painter, or the poet learns about *nature* from the rules of his art; without an intimate understanding of nature he can create nothing beautiful. The musician learns the rules of harmony

---

c He who specifically undertakes to write the history of instrumental music since Beethoven will no doubt have within this period to report on isolated phenomena, capable, assuredly, of arousing a particular and interested attention. But he who considers the history of the arts from a point of view as broad as is here necessary has to restrict himself to its chief moments alone; whatever departs from or derives from these moments he must leave out of account. And the more unmistakably such isolated phenomena reveal great talent, the more strikingly do precisely these phenomena prove—in view of the general sterility

of the whole artistic impulse behind them—that, once there has been expressed in their particular art variety what Beethoven expressed in music, whatever is left to be discovered has to do with technical procedures, perhaps, but not with the living spirit. In the great universal art work of the future it will be possible to keep on making new discoveries forever—but not in the individual art variety which, after having been conducted into universality as music was by Beethoven, perseveres in its isolated development.

3 An allusion to Mendelssohn's *Lobgesang.*

and counterpoint; his learning, without which he can erect no musical structure, is an abstract scientific system; attaining skill in its employment, he becomes a member of a guild and now, from the point of view of the guild member, looks into the world of actuality, which of necessity must seem a different world to *him* than to the worldly non-guild member— the *layman*. The uninitiated layman stands nonplused in turn before art music's artificial work, in which he quite correctly grasps nothing but what in general stirs his heart; this comes to him from out the marvelous structure solely in the form of melody immediately pleasing to the ear; everything else leaves him cold or disturbs him in a confused way, because he simply does not and cannot understand it. Our modern concert public, pretending to be satisfied and cordial toward the art symphony, is simply lying and dissembling, as we may verify at any moment if, after such a symphony—as is usual even in the most celebrated concert institutes—a melodious piece from any modern opera is played, for in this case we hear the real musical pulse of the auditorium beating at once with undissembled joy.

That there is any connection, conditioned by the public, between it and our art music must be flatly denied; wherever such a connection seeks to reveal itself, it is either affected and untrue or at least uncertain—as in the popular audience which occasionally succeeds in being carried away, without affectation, by the drastic side of a Beethoven symphony—and the impression made by these compositions is assuredly incomplete and fragmentary. Yet, where such a connection is lacking, the connection, as a guild, of the company of artists can be but superficial; the growth and shaping of art from within cannot be conditioned from out the artist community, which after all is mere artifice and system; only in the single artist, from out the individuality of the particular being, can there be active a natural impulse to shape and develop, governed by inner, instinctive laws. Denied its nourishment in external nature, the art-creative impulse can obtain it only in the peculiar character and abundance of an individual artist nature; only such an individuality—in its particularity, its personal view, its peculiar desiring, longing, and willing—can supply to the artistic substance the form-giving matter denied it in external nature; only in the individuality of this one particular human being does music become a purely human art; this individuality it consumes in order to attain, from out the fluidity of its very element, to concentration and to an individuality of its own.

Thus we see in music—as in the other arts, but for quite different reasons —that mannerism or so-called schools proceed as a rule exclusively from out the individuality of a particular artist. These schools were the guild companies which, in imitation, indeed in mimicry, grew up about a great master in whom was individualized the nature of the art. As long as music had not yet fulfilled its world-historical artistic task, the widespread branches of these schools, made fruitful by this or that relationship, could grow together as new seedlings; once this task had been completely fulfilled by the greatest of all musical individualities, once music from out its deepest abundance had through the force of this individuality destroyed the ultimate form in which it could remain an egoistically independent art —in a word, once *Beethoven* had written his last symphony—the musical guild companies could patch and mend to suit themselves in their effort to produce their absolute-musical man; from out their workshop there could now come forth only a patched and mended, pieced-together man of fantasy, not a sinuously stalwart man of nature. After Haydn and Mozart it was possible and necessary for a Beethoven to follow; music's genius needed him—without keeping music waiting, he was there; who now would be to Beethoven what he was to Haydn and Mozart in the realm of absolute music? Here the greatest genius could do nothing further, for the genius of absolute music has no further need for him.

You exert yourselves to no purpose when, to still your own childishly egoistic longing for productivity, you seek to deny the destructive, world-historical, musical significance of Beethoven's last symphony; not even the stupidity which enables you actually to misunderstand the work can save you! Do as you please; take no notice of Beethoven whatever, grope after Mozart, gird yourselves with Bach, write symphonies with or without voices, write masses, oratorios—those sexless operatic embryos!—make songs without words, operas without texts; you produce nothing that has real life in it. For behold—you do not have the *faith!*—the great faith in the necessity of what you do! You have only the faith of the foolish— the superstitious faith in the possibility of the necessity of your egoistic willfulness!

Surveying the busy desolation of our musical art world; becoming aware of the absolute impotence of this art substance, for all its eternal ogling of itself; viewing this shapeless mess, of which the dregs are the dried-up impertinence of pedantry, from which, for all its profoundly reflecting, ever-so-musical, self-arrogated mastery, can finally rise to the broad daylight of modern public life, as an artificially distilled stench, only emotionally dissolute Italian opera arias or impudent French cancan dance tunes; appraising, in short, this complete creative incapacity, we look about us fearlessly for the great destructive stroke of destiny which will put an end to all this immoderately inflated musical rubbish to make room for the art work of the future, in which genuine music will in truth assume no insignificant role, to which in this soil, however, air and room to breathe are peremptorily denied.[d]

. . . . .

FUNDAMENTALS OF THE ART WORK OF THE FUTURE

If we consider the situation of modern art—insofar as it is actually *art* —in relation to public life, we recognize first of all its complete inability to influence this public life in accordance with its high purpose. This is because, as a mere cultural product, it has not grown out of life, and because, as a hothouse plant, it cannot possibly take root in the natural soil and natural climate of the present. Art has become the exclusive property of an artist class; it gives pleasure only to those who *understand* it, requiring for its understanding a special study, remote from real life, the study of *art connoisseurship*. This study and the understanding it affords are thought today to be within the reach of everyone who has the money to pay for the art pleasures offered for sale; yet if we ask the artist whether the great multitude of our art amateurs are capable of understanding him in his highest flights, he can answer only with a deep sigh. And if he now reflects on the infinitely greater multitude of those who must remain cut off, as a result of the influence of our social conditions, unfavorable from every point of view, not only from the understanding, but even from the enjoyment of modern art, the artist of today cannot but become conscious that his whole artistic activity is, strictly speaking, only an egoistic self-complacent activity for activity's sake and that, in its relation to public life, his art is mere luxury, superfluity, and selfish pastime. The disparity, daily observed and bitterly deplored, between so-called culture and the lack of it is so monstrous, a mean between them so unthinkable, their reconciliation so impossible, that, granted a minimum of honesty, the modern art based on this unnatural culture would have to admit, to its deepest shame, that

---

d Lengthily as I have spoken here about the nature of music, in comparison with the other art varieties (a procedure fully justified, I may add, by the peculiar character of music and by the peculiar and truly productive developmental process resulting from this character), I am well aware of the many-sided incompleteness of my discussion; not one book, however, but many books would be needed to lay bare exhaustively the immorality, the weakness, the meanness of the ties connecting our modern music and our modern life; to explore the unfortunate overemotional side of music, which makes it subject to the speculation of our education maniacs, our "improvers of the people," who seek to mix the honey of music with the vinegar-sourish sweat of the mistreated factory worker as the one possible mitigation of his sufferings (somewhat as our sages of the state and bourse are at pains to stuff the servile rags of religion into the gaping holes in the policeman's care of society); and finally to explain the saddening psychological phenomenon that a man may be not only cowardly and base, but also *stupid*, without these qualities preventing him from being a perfectly respectable musician.

it owed its existence to a life element which in turn could base *its* existence only on the utter lack of culture in the real mass of humanity. The one thing that, in this, its allotted situation, modern art should be able to do —and, where there is honesty, does endeavor to do—namely, *to further the diffusion of culture*—it cannot do, for the simple reason that art, to have any influence on life, must be itself the flowering of a *natural* culture —that is, of one that has grown up from below—and can never be in a position to rain down culture from above. At best, then, our cultured art resembles the speaker who seeks to communicate with a people in a language which it does not understand—all that he says, his most ingenious sayings above all, can lead only to the most laughable confusions and misunderstandings.

Let us first make apparent how modern art is to proceed if it would attain *theoretically* to the redemption of its uncomprehended self from out its isolated situation and to the widest possible understanding of the public; how this redemption can become possible only through the *practical* mediation of the public will then be readily apparent of itself.

·   ·   ·   ·   ·

Man as artist can be fully satisfied only in the union of all the art varieties in the *collective* art work; in every *individualization* of his artistic capacities he is *unfree*, not wholly that which he can be; in the collective art work he is *free*, wholly that which he can be.

The *true* aim of art is accordingly *all-embracing;* everyone animated by the true artistic impulse seeks to attain, through the full development of his particular capacity, not the glorification of *this particular capacity*, but the glorification *in art of mankind in general*.

The highest collective art work is the *drama;* it is present in its *ultimate completeness* only when *each art variety, in its ultimate completeness,* is present in it.

True drama can be conceived only as resulting from the *collective impulse of all the arts* to communicate in the most immediate way with a *collective public;* each individual art variety can reveal itself as *fully understandable* to this collective public only through collective communication, together with the other art varieties, in the drama, for the aim of each individual art variety is fully attained only in the mutually understanding and understandable co-operation of all the art varieties.

·   ·   ·   ·   ·

Not *one* of the richly developed capacities of the individual arts will remain unused in the collective art work of the future; it is precisely in the collective art work that these capacities will attain to full stature. Thus especially the art of tone, developed with such singular diversity in instrumental music, will realize in the collective art work its richest potentialities—will indeed incite the pantomimic art of dancing in turn to wholly new discoveries and inspire the breath of poetry no less to an undreamed-of fullness. For in its isolation music has formed itself an organ capable of the most immeasurable expression—the *orchestra.* Beethoven's tonal language, introduced through the orchestra into the drama, is a force wholly new to the dramatic art work. If architecture and, still more so, scenic landscape painting can place the dramatic actor in the natural environment of the physical world and give him, from the inexhaustible font of natural phenomena, a background constantly rich and relevant, the orchestra—that animate body of infinite harmonic variety— offers the individual actor, as a support, what may be called a perpetual source of the natural element of man as artist. The orchestra is, so to speak, the soil of infinite universal feeling from which the individual feeling of the single actor springs into full bloom; it somehow dissolves the solid motionless floor of the actual scene into a fluid, pliant, yielding, impressionable, ethereal surface whose unfathomed bottom is the sea of feeling itself. Thus the orchestra resembles the *earth,* from which *Antaeus,* once he touched it with his feet, gathered renewed and deathless vital energy. Although by nature diametrically opposed to the actor's natural scenic environment and hence, as local color, placed very rightly in the deepened foreground outside the scenic frame, it also constitutes the perfect complement of scenic environment, expanding the inexhaustible natural element of the *physical* world to the no less inexhaustible emotional element of *man* as artist; this composite element encircles the actor as with an atmospheric elemental ring of nature and of art; in this he moves assured, as do the heavenly bodies, in ultimate completeness, at the same time sending forth in all directions his views and feelings, endlessly expanded, as do the heavenly bodies their rays, into the infinite distances.

Thus completing one another in their ever-changing round, the united sister arts will show themselves and bring their influence to bear, now collectively, now two at a time, now singly, as called for by the need of the dramatic action, the one determinant of aim and measure. At one moment plastic pantomime will listen to thought's dispassionate appraisal; at another the will of resolute thought will overflow into the immediate expression of gesture; at still another music will have to utter the flood of feeling, the awe of apprehension; finally, however, all three, in mutual entwinement, will exalt the will of drama to immediate active deed. For there is one thing which all three united art varieties must will, would they be free to act—this is the *drama;* all three must be concerned for the attainment of the dramatic aim. If they are conscious of this aim, if all direct their will to its accomplishment, each will receive the strength to lop off on all sides the egoistic offshoots of its particular nature from the common trunk, in order that the tree may grow, not shapelessly in all directions, but to the proud summit of its branches, twigs, and leaves—to its crown.

Human nature, like the art variety, is in itself multiform and many-sided; the soul of the *individual* man—the activity most necessary to him, his strongest instinctive urge—is a *single* thing. If he recognizes this single thing as his basic nature, he can, to further its indispensable attainment, suppress each weaker, subordinate desire, each feeble longing whose satisfaction might hinder him in this attainment. Only the weak and impotent man discovers in himself no supremely strong and necessary soul's desire; at every moment he is subject to chance appetite, stirred up incidentally from without; precisely because this is mere appetite, he can never satisfy it; tossed willfully back and forth from one appetite to another, he never even attains to real enjoyment. But if this man, knowing no need, has might enough obstinately to pursue the satisfaction of these chance appetites, then there arise in life and art those horrible and monstrous phenomena which—as excrescences of mad egoistic impulses, as murderous debaucheries of despots, or as lascivious modern operas—fill us with such unspeakable disgust. If, on the other hand, the individual man discovers in himself a strong desire, an urge repressing every other longing that he feels, in other words, that necessary inner impulse which makes up his soul and being, and if he bends all his energy to satisfy it, then he exalts his might, and with it his particular capacity, to a strength and height he cannot otherwise attain.

The individual man, given perfect health of body, heart, and mind, can experience no higher need than that common to all men similarly constituted, for, as a *real* need, it can only be such as he can satisfy in the community alone. But the strongest and most necessary need of the perfect artist is to communicate himself in the ultimate completeness of his being to the ultimate community, and he attains this with the universal intelligibility necessary to it only in the *drama*. In the drama he expands his particular being to general being by representing an individual personality other than his own. He must wholly forget himself to comprehend another personality with the completeness necessary to representation; he attains this only when he explores this individuality with such precision in its contact, penetration, and completion with and by other individualities—hence also the being of these other individualities themselves—when he apprehends this individuality so accurately that it is possible for him to become conscious of this contact, penetration, and completion in his own being; the perfect representative artist is therefore the individual expanded to the *being of the species* in accordance with the ultimate completion of his own particular being. The scene in which this wondrous process is accomplished is the *theatrical stage;* the collective art work which it brings to light is the *drama.* To force his particular being to the highest flowering of its content in this *one* highest art work, the individual artist, however, like the individual art variety, has to repress each willful egoistic inclination to untimely expansion useless to the whole in order to be able to contribute the more actively to the attainment of the highest collective aim, which is in turn not to be realized without the individual and his periodic limitation.

This aim—the aim of the drama—is at the same time the only genuinely artistic aim that can be possibly *realized;* whatever is remote from it must necessarily lose itself in the sea of the uncertain, the unintelligible, the unfree. And this aim is attained, not by *one art variety for itself alone,*[e] but only by *all collectively,* and therefore the *most universal* art work is at the same time the one art work that is real and free—in other words, universally *intelligible.*

. . . . .

---

e The modern *playwright* will be the one least inclined to admit that the drama is not to belong exclusively even to *his* art variety, the *art of poetry;* in particular he will be unable to persuade himself to share the drama with the tone poet— or, as he would put it, to allow the play to be absorbed by the opera. As long as the opera exists, the play—and, with as much right, the pantomime —will unquestionably continue to exist also; as long as argument on this point is thinkable, the drama of the future will remain unthinkable. If, however, the poet's doubts lie deeper, and he objects that he cannot understand how *singing* is once and for all to take over the place of spoken dialogue, the reply will be that, in two respects, he has not yet come to a clear understanding as to the character of the art work of the future. In the first place, he does not stop to consider that music, in this art work, is to be given a place altogether different from its place in the modern opera; that it is to unfold its full breadth only where its capacity is greatest, while, in all places where dra-matic speech, for example, is what is needed most, it is to subordinate itself completely to this; and that music, without becoming altogether silent, has the capacity to adapt itself to the thoughtful element of speech so imperceptibly that, while supporting speech, it scarcely interferes with it at all. Having recognized this, the poet has in the second place to realize that those ideas and situations, in connection with which even the slightest and most restrained support of music must seem burdensome and importunate, can arise only from the spirit of the modern play, a spirit which, in the art work of the future, will find no further breathing space whatever. The man whom the drama of the future will represent has no longer anything at all to do with that prosaic intriguing hodgepodge, dictated by state and fashion, which our modern poets have so circumstantially to tangle and untangle; his action and speech, dictated by nature, is Yes and No; all else is evil, that is, modern and superfluous.

Index